Muddle Your Way Through Being a Grandparent

■ ■ ■

How To Fool People Into Thinking You're A Competent Granny Or Grandpa

Paul Merrill

Praise for *A Polar Bear Ate My Head* by Paul Merrill

This is the hilarious and surreal true story of Britain's biggest ever men's magazine launch... and the chaos and disasters that followed

Paul Merrill was an award-winning magazine editor when he was inexplicably chosen to launch Britain's first weekly publication aimed at the 'new lad': ZOO. He quickly gained notoriety after running competitions to find the country's randiest nanna, ugliest baby and teen mum of the year, and offering prizes of a boob job for your girlfriend, lesbian wedding and even euthanasia.

Then he was suddenly deported to Australia to launch ZOO there, and events became even more outlandish.

Find out how Merrill:

- attacked Tony Blair with a puppet
- lost 130,000 pairs of inflatable breasts in the South China Sea
- accidentally gave his home address to a serial killer
- tried to cook a dwarf
- threw a biscuit at Christopher Lee
- searched for the hottest horse dentist and sexiest wall.
- employed Mo Mowlam as a sex columnist
- was accused by the attorney general of trying to overthrow the government
- persuaded the Aussie prime minister's daughter to strip off
- was given advice on stain removal by Gordon Brown
- received death threats by enraged Islamists and a convicted killer

Containing hundreds of bizarre and unexpected anecdotes, A Polar Bear Ate My Head is the most side-splitting insider's account of

Also in this series

Muddle Your Way Through Fatherhood
How to fool people into thinking you're a competent dad.

Available from Amazon.com

Contents

To my mum and dad, who muddled less than I do

1

Are you ready to be a grandparent?

"Never have children, only grandchildren."

Gore Vidal

"I want to die in my sleep like my grandfather — not screaming and yelling like the passengers in his car."

Will Shriner

Wow! You're going to be a grandparent. And at your age too. You hardly look old enough.

Actually – who are we kidding - you *do* look old enough. Mainly because you *are* old enough to have a child who is old enough to have sex. That's the only real qualification required for grandparent-hood.

But it's possible you don't *feel* old enough. When you were young, grannies and grandpas were white-haired, stooped old grouches who needed their meals liquidized and their mattresses protected by a waterproof cover.

That's not you, is it?

You're not wizened and befuddled with age. And even if you are, you probably don't realize it, which is a blessing.

This book, then, is for the new breed of grandparents, who aren't 'little old ladies'. Or even little old men. Yes, you are of a senior generation, and yes, you've seen better days*, but you refuse to be written off as 'elderly' or 'geriatric' or 'muddled' even though there's a chance you're all three.

After all, unlike *your* grandparents, you experienced the Summer of Love**, Beatlemania and Woodstock, so there's little that can shock you.

You see 'young people today' (a useful phrase to contemptuously dismiss anyone under forty) think they know it all, and that you have served your purpose by procreating, rearing and amassing enough of an inheritance to provide them a new kitchen once you fall off your mortal coil.

What could an oldie like you possibly teach them? You may have spent a lifetime gaining experience and knowledge, and have brought up your own children, but now those children are adults, if they need some advice, do they come to you?

Do they heck. If they need to know something, they just Google it. Which is the same as asking a complete stranger who may, for all they know, be a childless, serial killing Nazi cult leader. And we can only imagine the horrors that may be caused by acting on advice from someone who's actually *childless*.

Anyway, the point is, you are about to find out that being a grandparent isn't a walk in the park these days. It's more like a walk in a safari park with packs of toothy predators waiting to pounce and gobble up your wrinkled hide if you're not on your guard.

Think I'm being overdramatic in a blatant attempt to get you to buy this book? That you're better off with one of those well-meaning books with a cute-as-a-button kid on the cover being cuddled by an old person? (Not in an Operation Yewtree way, you understand). Well fine, purchase one of those and see where it gets you.

Whoa! I was being sarcastic. Put it back on the shelf and back away slowly.

That was close.

Now you have actual grandchildren, on a mission to exploit your kindness, digestives and burgeoning dementia.

So you need a book that will arm you with all the, er, arms you need to survive in today's brutal grandparenting landscape. A book that dares to tell you things the other books don't want you to know, and isn't afraid to open your eyes to the hidden landmines that pepper your way ***

One…oh, let's see, well, a bit like *this* one.

Yes, this is the book they tried to hush up. The book they wanted banned. The book that could be very dangerous in the wrong hands. If Wikileaks really want to expose the truth, they could do worse than start right here **** For this publication is the only truly honest account of how your life is about to change and the only one equipping you with all the lies, excuses and threats you're going to need over the coming years.

But hang on a second. There's a small chance that I'm creating the impression that being a grandma or granddad is a bad thing, which of course it isn't.

It's good. In fact it's great. All I'm saying is that you have a lot to consider. And luckily, literally *all* the answers to the questions rattling around your addled brain are contained within these pages. If it's not covered off here, it's not worth knowing.

So if you're still browsing, you're wasting valuable time. Right now a ticking time bomb is, er, ticking and when it goes off (or, more accurately, comes out) you are going to need to be ready. And if *you're* the one with the bomb inside you, buy this for your folks, stuff it through their letterbox (the book, not the bomb) and retire to a safe distance.

* And several better decades

** Followed by the Autumn of Antibiotics

*** I think we've moved on from the safari analogy, as toothy predators wandering around might actually be useful if you are worried about landmines.

**** Although technically it hasn't been banned as I write. Maybe because I haven't really started it yet. However, trust no one. Except me. But then I would say that.

Will you be a good grandparent?

This is probably a question you've never considered. After all, you brought up your own kids, and being a grandparent can't be more difficult than that, right?

Well, yes. And no. On the plus side, it's only a part time gig, but on the minus side, you're now old, infirm and more easily confused.

So, let's start by taking this handy quiz to see just how potentially terrible you're going to be....

1. Can you knit?
    Yes, and the bootees are already underway (+ 5 points)
    Yes, but the bootees at Oxfam are only £3 and can be passed off as my own (+ 1 point)
    No, knitting is for old people. Oh, wait.. (- 5 points)

2. The most precious day of your life was:
    A   The day you had your first born (+ 4 points)
    B   The day your last born finally moved out (-2 points)
    C   The day Scott married Charlene in Neighbours (-3 points)

3. On an average day, which profanities do you utter?
    Heavens to Betsy (+ 6 points)
    Lord luv a duck (+ 4 points)
    Goodness gracious me (+2 points)
    Fiddlesticks (+1 point)
    Oh, bother (-1 point)
    Oh f***, the stupid c*** is screaming it's a*** off again (-2 points)

4. Corporal punishment is...

A   Not as effective as setting clear boundaries (+ 7 points)

B   Only used as a last resort (+ 1 point)

C   Fine if it's only a light smack with a slipper (-1 point)

D   What keeps our sex life alive (-4 points)

E   Not as effective as waterboarding (-10 points)

5. As soon as the baby arrives you will..

   A   Be available to rock it to sleep and help with the washing (+ 8 point)

   B   Expect to be invited over before the other grandparents (-1 point)

   C   Fake the SARS virus to avoid babysitting

6. When you are handed the baby for the first time, you will say...

   A   Aah, the miracle of life. Bless you my child (+6 points)

   B   Aah, I'm sure he'll grow into his face (-7 points)

   C   Aah, he's got Great Uncle Ernie's lazy eye (- 2 points)

   D   Aagh! oh Jeez, what the...? Whoa, take that thing away (-10 points)

7. Your greatest hope for your grandchild is:

   A   That they live a long and fulfilled life (+ 11 points)

   B   That they end up down the mines like your Fred. If it was good enough for him... (-6 points)

   C   That they win the lottery and buy you a house by the sea. (- 3 points)

   D   That they make more of their life than their layout, deadbeat parents (-4 points)

8. Your house is:

   A   A quaint rose-covered cottage with flock wallpaper, flying ducks on the wall and a Victoria sponge cooling on the windowsill. (+ 13 points)

B   Part of a hippy commune of free love, lentils and hash cakes every other Thursday (-2 points)

C   Walthamstow crack den littered with old needles, dead junkies and spoons (- 12 points)

9.   The first thing you do in the morning is:

A   Get your husband or wife a nice cuppa and the newspaper to read in bed (+ 6 points)

B   Call for the nurse and tell her that your hot water bottle has turned into a Portuguese man o' war again.

C   Check the gun's still under the pillow and the money's gone from the mantelpiece (-5 points)

10.   The best advice you can offer your grandchildren as they grow up is:

A   Follow your dreams and clean your teeth (+ 3 points)

B   Never eat yellow snow (0 points)

C   If you dump a body at sea, puncture the stomach so it doesn't float (-13 points)

+ 10 and over

There's a chance you'll make a decent grandparent. But only if you read this book. Failure to do so will result in the subtraction of fifty points from your score.

-10 to +9

You somehow managed to raise your own kids, but possibly not well. You are going to have to be careful to avoid unwarranted attention from social services.

-11 and below

You have the grandparenting skills of a frozen turkey. Read this book twice before handling grandchildren.

How to avoid a dud son or daughter-in-law

The fact you're reading this book, may make this section redundant. If your idiot child has already impregnated (or been impregnated by) someone of whom you disapprove, there's very little you can do. And by 'very little', I of course mean 'nothing'.

However, if that hasn't happened but you suspect it will, there is still time to gently guide them into making the right choice. It's a decision they will have to live with for the rest of their lives. Or until the decree nisi. And then it'll be you who will be expected to pick up the pieces and pretend that no one could have foreseen their loved one turn into a psychotic philanderer.

So, you may need to act quickly. If he/she brings home a ludicrously stupid choice of partner, don't merely point out how ludicrously stupid they are as this will antagonize them. It'll also antagonize the ludicrously stupid one if they are within earshot.

Instead, be subtle. Deep down they do still want your approval, so you can use that against them if you need to. In the meantime, try dropping a few of these 'innocent' phrases into the conversation. But do be subtle. If you use all ten within thirty seconds, they may get wise to your scheme. Good luck!

1. Sandra's lovely, and just think - all your kids will be redheads.
2. You're so handsome, you could have had any woman you want, and yet you've chosen Liz. I'm so proud.
3. Yes, I know her daddy paid for her to go to Harvard, but if a hippo lives in a stable, it doesn't make it a horse.
4. Of course I like Darren, and I hear he wants to have at least eight children.
5. He's quite a find, dear. And with a nose that size, you can get your kids to sniff out truffles.
6. I agree he's adorable. And I bet you can't wait to be Mrs Cockrot, can you?

7. Always look at a woman's mother to see what she'll be like when she's older. Oh, and did you ever find that remote control you lost in Fiona's mum's rolls of fat?

8. I know he only carried out the armed robbery to buy you an engagement ring. And it'll be such a special Christmas for us all when he gets parole in 2032.

9. I've nothing against Nigel wearing flamboyant shirts. I just said I was a bit worried when he made a pass at your dad.

10. Well I don't think it's unreasonable to ask you to wear this chastity belt until you see sense and realise he's not going to leave The Rolling Stones and marry you.

Of course, the other danger is that if they meet a half decent partner, that you will express your approval too strongly. Not everyone wants to be with someone if their parents like them. So tread carefully, while simultaneously doing everything in your power to make sure they stay together.

Reverse psychology may be your friend here. Try a few of these:

1. You really like Peter? Won't you get bored by all those holidays on his father's yacht in St Tropez?

2. I suppose Catherine is okay if you like the supermodel type.

3. Don't you want to wait until you find someone more like your father?

4. I'm warning you now - if you marry her, I'm afraid you're going to end up being saddled with our Mercedes.

5. It's really not fair if you marry Stephen – all your friends will be madly jealous, and you don't want that, do you?

6. He's all right for a chiseled multi-millionaire philanthropist, I guess. But will being rich beyond your wildest dreams really make you happier than finding a nice local farm boy?

If all of this doesn't work and they make a tragically appalling choice of mate, then, beyond organizing a contract killing, you are going to have to lump it. Your parents probably didn't approve of your choice, did they? And you survived. Just about.

Anyway, as we'll see later on, there are still ways you can have an influence and make sure that they don't totally screw up your grandchildren. All is not lost. And, who knows, you may grow to like their choice. Maybe he/she has hidden talents, a caring nature or a large penis. Though the latter is not a talent you want your son to discover on his wedding night.

2

The announcement
(and how to mask your horror)

"Becoming a grandmother is wonderful. One moment you're just a mother. The next you are all-wise and prehistoric."

Pam Brown

I used to be with it. But then they changed what it was. Now what I'm with isn't it, and what's it seems scary and weird. It'll happen to you.

Abe Simpson

Being told out of the blue that you're about to become grandparents can be either a wondrous surprise, or worse than being informed that you need to have your colon removed.

So it's important that you handle it in the right way. Especially if all those tips in the last chapter to get your grown up child to date the right person failed abysmally. Which, let's be honest, is quite possible.

Your initial response may be one of genuine shock caused by realisation that:

1. Your child has actually had sex with this person.
2. You're older than you were twenty years ago.

Obviously the magic of the occasion is lessened slightly if your daughter is still at school or borstal and if their chosen life partner is the balding forty-eight-year-old school bus driver who still wears a Def Leppard t-shirt.

But a new baby is still magical, even if half his genes are from a lower life form.

The first thing to do is hug. During the embrace, your son or daughter won't be able to see the gritted-teeth smile which has formed on your face. Hold them tightly for a few seconds while you work on making it seem an expression of real joy. If this takes more than two minutes, release your grip as it might feel more like a headlock by now.

Remember that this thing is going to happen whether you like it or not. So if you really cannot say anything positive, say something that *sounds* positive, but is actually non-committal. Things like:

Wow, I can hardly believe it's true
That really is news, isn't it?
You must both be thrilled
Gosh, I'm glad I've already taken my Valium
I'm sure the other grandparents will be so much more excited than we are

A few recent surveys have* revealed that middle class families don't always react as well as the working class in such circumstances. Perhaps they have higher expectations or are simply utter snobs.

Here are two realistic scenarios to illustrate this point, and show how the occasion can go a bit wrong if you're not careful.

* *Might* have

Scenario 1: Middle class

It was a typical Sunday afternoon for Mr and Mrs Fortesque. Petunia was dusting the chandelier while Reginald was pruning his roses. The doorbell heralds the arrival of their 24-year-old daughter, Geraldine with her boyfriend, Spike.

Reginald	Ah, hello, lovely to see you. Come in and I'll put the kettle on.
Geraldine:	Yeah, hi, dad, look, can we…
Reginald:	I was just telling your mum that..
Geraldine:	Dad…
Reginald:	Yes, love
Geraldine:	Oh…nothing. Is Mum in because we've got something…
Petunia:	Darling! How marvelous. Oh, and Thingy too I see.
Geraldine:	His name is Spike
Petunia:	Yes, well, come in and sit down and we'll get some tea in the pot
Geraldine:	Yeah, thanks. Look, Mum, there's…
Petunia:	Did you hear that, Reginald? *Reginald!* REGINALD! Oh, there you are, dear. Three teas, and get those short-bread fingers too. Now what was it you were saying?
Geraldine:	Maybe we should wait for Dad.
Petunia:	Ooh, sounds exciting! Have you got another promotion at work?
Geraldine:	shakes her head.
Petunia:	Oh, well surely Spike hasn't finally got a job, has he?
Geraldine:	Mum! Leave him alone. You know how difficult it is for poets to get published. No, what I wanted to tell you is that we're…
Reginald:	Tea up! Now you take two sugars, don't you, Spike?
Spike:	Yeah, cheers, man
Petunia:	Mrs Rowbottom was only telling me yesterday that the garden centre needs people to dig the beds. And…

Geraldine: He's not a labourer, Mum. He's a writer.

Petunia: Well, whatever. In my day, you got whatever job you could get. My father always said…

Geraldine   Oh for God's sake, Mum…. I'm pregnant!

Stunned silence, sound of shortbread finger falling to the carpet.

Reginald   Oh God.

Petunia: No, no, no. You're not. You can't be. Not with… I mean, are you sure? I thought I was pregnant once, before I had you, and it was just a spot of, er. Maybe you're just…

Geraldine   No, it's definite. I'm three months gone.

Reginald: Oh God

Petunia: But why darling? Why now? Why with… (starts to cry) This can't be true.

Spike: I've bought a cot for it.

More silence

Petunia (still in tears): This is all your fault, Reginald. How many times did I tell you that she needed to go to finishing school? But no, it had to be university. Well now look. I hope you're satisfied.

Geraldine: Look, we're in love and very happy. So…

Petunia: Happy? How can you be happy? What will the ladies at church say? Have you considered that? Mrs Blooming-ton-Smyth will have a field day, I can tell you. A baby! I can hardly believe it. And with… Oh the shame

Spike: I thought I'd paint it blue

Petunia: What? Paint the baby blue?

Spike: The cot

Petunia: Oh shut up, will you. And how, may I ask, do you propose to provide for a child? You're pathetic.

Geraldine: Mum, that's it. I'm sick of your attitude to me. I happen to love this man (points to Spike, who shrugs shoulders and smiles awkwardly).

Petunia: Love? Hah!

Geraldine: I don't need you in my life if you can't accept him. And you won't be seeing your grandchild any time soon. Come on, love, we're leaving.

Reginald   Oh God

Scenario 2: Working class

It's a typical Monday afternoon for Mr and Mrs Miggins. Shaz has just lit up her 23rd roll up of the day while Bert is cleaning out the pigeon cage. The doorbell heralds the arrival of their 24-year-old daughter, Sharonbert and her boyfriend, Nobby.

Bert: You get me fags?
Sharonbert: Nah, ma benefit's all gone. I think Nobby put it on the dogs last night, didn't yer, love?
Nobby: What if I did?
Shaz: What you want, anyway? Can't you see I'm reading *Take a Break*?
Sharonbert: I'm pregnant
Shaz: So? What d'ya want me to do about it?
Bert (to Nobby): Is it yours then?
Nobby: Dunno. Might be. Might not be.
Sharonbert: Anyway, thought you might wanna know.
Bert (to Nobby): You got any smokes on yer?
Nobby: Not for you, ya lazy f***er.
Bert: Just gizz us one.
Sharonbert: Nah, give it me, I need one more than 'im.
Shaz: Well you can all shut it, WAG Nation's starting.
Sharonbert: Dad, get us a Special Brew from the fridge will yer. I'm eatin' fer two now, innit.

These two scenes skillfully prove the point without resorting to crude class stereotypes or offensive clichés. We can see that the middle classes are a bunch of toffee-nosed, stuck up monsters, while the working class are more grounded, more in control and more drunk.

How to mask your horror

The point is, when you're told the news, you will feel a heady mixture of emotions pulsing through your brain, and actual speech may not be possible for a few seconds. Which is a good thing because it gives you time to get a hold on what has just happened, and how you are going to respond. Just remember not to articulate *exactly* what you're thinking.

Stick this handy list of useful phrases on the fridge in readiness and pluck one to say.

What you'll think: But you're only 14. You've thrown the rest of your life away, I wash my hands of you
What to say: Experiencing parenthood this early will make you more rounded and better person.

What you'll think: You're having a kid with a prisoner on death row in The States, who strangled his own granny???
What you'll say: Maybe this little miracle can bring some compassion and meaning to an individual who has lost his way.

What you'll think: For Christ's sake, if your boyfriend is Chinese, don't you think your husband will realise it's not his?
What to say: This little blessing will help us all think about our lives and who we really want to spend them with

What you'll think: I'm thrilled you're expecting, but, for the love of God, you cannot call my grandson OJ Tyson Smith
What you'll say: That's a lovely idea, so memorable. But don't rush the decision, there is plenty of time to look at all options.

What you'll think: Wonderful news, dear, but you can't seriously be suggesting that we'll join you in eating the placenta.

What you'll say: Thank you so much for wanting us involved in such a special way. If we hadn't agreed to go to Aunt Myrtle's whist drive, we'd be there like a shot

What you'll think: But we're Amish, you're supposed to be a virgin
What to say: That's lovely, but let me just go back to work in the fields for a few hours to work out how I'll square it with our people

What you'll think: How is that even possible? You're pushing 50
What to say: God moves in mysterious and wonderful ways. Not usually *this* mysterious, mind.

What you'll think: Sextuplets? But you live in a bedsit
What to say: My, looks like you'll all have to move in with us. How lucky we are. Don't worry, we can get some of the money back on the round the world cruise

What you'll think: Let me see if I've got this right - you can't remember his name, what he looks like, or in what position he players for the Over 45s 2nds?
What to say: The baby will always be surrounded by love, even if the father's not there. But, equally, let's hope it wasn't the ex-con prop with the hairy knuckles and cleft palate.

Whatever you choose to say can't change the fact that this baby is on its way. Even now it is plotting its escape and has probably already sniffed out your biscuit tin.

Becoming a grandparent was always going to be a shock to the system, to the fact you've survived it without any palpitations is a good sign. And there will be lots more palpitations to further test your cardiovascular system, perhaps even making it stronger.

Perhaps.

But while you're wasting time reading this, there's a lot you need to be getting on with. After all the baby will be here in only a few months and there's so much more you need to do to prepare than you could ever imagine. Islanders in the path of a category 5 hurricane have less to worry about.

So come on – stop reading this and start on the next chapter before this metaphorical wind system takes you unawares.

Skip this final sentence to save time.

3

Preparing for the onslaught

"One of life's greatest mysteries is how the boy who wasn't good enough to marry your daughter can be the father of the smartest grandchild in the world."

Jewish proverb

"Just about the time a woman thinks her work is done, she becomes a grandmother."

Edward H. Dreschnack

What sort of grandparent will you be?

Ok, you're over the initial shock, coming to terms with the fact that you are officially not young, and it's time to think about all the wondrous ways in which your life will change.

Just as you finally got the kids to move out, suddenly they're about to ruin everything all over again. And just as you'd got that lovely cream carpet and swapped the black Labrador for a white poodle. Luckily, you've got this book to guide you past the many landmines ahead. That's two bomb metaphors, and we're barely into Chapter 3. Not a good omen.

But, hang on. You're being very negative about this. You always wanted grandkids, right? Good, so let's look on the bright side. If you're careful, they might not ruin *everything*. You can still have a life, of sorts. There will be the odd day here and there where *you* can decide what you'd like to do. And having little 'uns around will keep you feeling youthful, won't it?

Yes – youthful and completely knackered. Or, more accurately, old and completely knackered, but *feeling* a bit younger than you would have if you'd lived alone and had never had children.

And, of course, feeling a bit poorer too as bringing up kids has left you on the cusp of poverty.

So, as you await the arrival, you have plenty of time to work out what sort of grandparent you will be. Loving? Caring? Wise? Grumpy? Homicidal?

Sometimes it helps to think of a well-known old person who you admire, and make them your role model. But who to choose?

Start by answer these five questions to see if it helps you decide…

1. Your grandchildren are coming over for tea. You serve them:
    A   Home made scones with lashings of ginger beer
    B   Rohypnol

2. It's bedtime and they want a story. You read them:
    A   Charlotte's Web
    B   Vera Drake

3. For their birthday, you will give them:
    A   A chunky jumper you've knitted
    B   Their own cell

4. You catch one of them scrumping apples from next door's garden. You:
    A   Make them return the apples and apologise.
    B   Chain them up in the cellar and let your husband dole out the punishment

5. You can tell your daughter is run off her feet. To help her out, you:
    A   Pop over and do a little housework
    B   Start digging a shallow grave

Mostly As: Your role model is any rosy-cheeked old granny sitting in a rocking chair by the fireside and baking cakes. Sort of like Miss Marple, except she never actually had kids as such, but you get the idea. Lovely, polite, comforting, and possibly able to solve murders. Your grandchildren will adore you

Mostly Bs: Your role model is Rose West. In fact you may even be Rose West. Try to act natural.

That probably didn't help much. But, if you did opt for mostly Bs, at least you're no longer under no illusions that you're going to win Granny of the Year. Especially not after they find the bodies.

What should they call me?

Another thing you need to consider at this point is what name you'll be saddled with by your grandchild when it learns to speak. Don't let it choose something itself or else you'll end up being Nonny and Popsy for the next thirty years.

Here are some alternatives:

Grandmother – Formal, grand and sounds a bit Victorian. You'll be cold, unfeeling and matronly.

Grandmamma – Only if you live in Downton Abbey.

Grandma – Usually you'll be too late for this one as the other grandmother will have established first dibs on it well before conception took place.

Granny – Suggests you're older, possibly more wrinkly and therefore infirm.

Nan – Bit of a down market choice. Sounds more like someone who works on the wet fish counter in Sainsbury's rather than a precious member of the extended family

Nanny – Acceptable option for old goats, no one else.

Big Mom – Not a good idea unless you and your son are both gangsta rappers. Even then a poor choice.

Grammy – a bit too close to 'gammy'.

G-Ma – A possibility if you're under thirty with special needs.

Pa – Ideal for the grandchild with a speech impediment as most kids, and even some dolphins, can manage it.

Gramps – Quite close to grumps. You'll be a Clint Eastwood-style grandfather, meaning well, but still chewing tobacco.

Grandad – old, dithering, confused. Also prone to wandering.

Pops – More informal and bit more chummy, but suggests a grandparent who hasn't accepted that he's ancient enough to have two generations below him.

Gumpy – A Gumpy would certainly be fun, but is also an awkward mix of Gummy and guppy.

Grandaddy – Very posh and a bit austere. Would like his grandchildren to be presented to him for a formal inspection like Baron Von Trapp

Papadaddy – Sounds vaguely Italian or like a character from Nickelodeon. Also embarrassing to eventually be called this by adult grandchildren.

Big D – Conveys authority. . .and obesity

Readying your house for demolition

Yes, the birth may be some way off, but now isn't the time to be in denial about what is about to happen. Once this thing enters the world, it will be brought round to your house for inspection and the potential for widespread destruction is immediate. So don't wait until the thing is sitting smugly in its carrycot in your front room eyeing vulnerable items, act now.

Grandchildren very quickly develop a nasty habit of assuming they are welcome in your house at any time. This is fine when all they can do it sit in a playpen and occasionally vomit over the carpet or poke the dog's eye, but it becomes trickier when they develop muscle tone in their legs and can actually crawl or, worse, walk around.

The Chinese had the best antidote to this in binding feet to make movement more difficult. But modern day parents generally don't welcome this suggestion.

Instead you have to urgently adapt your beautiful home to make it child-safe all over again. The main concern here isn't so much the child's safety (kids usually heal after a bit), it's to minimise the number of your possessions that are obliterated.

A baby who has just learned to toddle can be a cocky bugger – showing off their new mobility with scant regard for your ornaments and plate glass table.

Such a child needs to be treated like a tsunami. It will surge in and destroy everything that is not safely stored above three feet.

In fact a good way to ascertain whether you have made everything safe is to organize an actual influx of water. Once it has receded, you can easily see which items were left too low and throw them out.

Main things to consider are:

A   Glass and china are much more fun to play with then plastic

B   Wiping a dirty mouth on a bib isn't as convenient as wiping it on a white shag pile or suede sofa.

C   Toys on wheels can be pushed faster across a sitting room than Sabastien Vettel in his Red Bull F1 car.

D   Nothing beats putting small objects into their mouths, preferably a few at a time.

E   In the time it takes you to glance round at the clock to see where the hell your son is, it's possible for a baby to equal the land speed record and be half way up the stairs chasing the cat.

It was, of course, different when you were bringing up *your* kids. The worst they could get up to was to chew on a fallen asbestos roof tile or steal one of your thalidomide tablets. And what harm did it ever do them?

Should you learn to knit?

No, you shouldn't, not under any circumstances. Because even if you lived to four hundred and thirty-five, life would still be too short.

Nor should you learn to smelt metal, build dry stone walls or speak Arabic as there are already people who do it. Leave it to them.

The birth of grandchildren is not the time to learn a complex new skill. Just think old dogs, new tricks. All your *old* tricks are so much more useful than any new ones would be.

That said, the image of a slightly tubby grandma rocking in her armchair knitting a sweet cardigan for her granddaughter and listening to Glenn Miller is still appealing.

But spending hours laboriously knitting and pearling is no fun for anyone, and there's a clear and present danger that by the time you finish the garment, the child will already be shaving.

So if you do feel the need to fulfill the knitting gran cliché, you are going to need to fake it.

Firstly go to a charity shop and buy some cheap, hand-knitted goods. Then find someone who *can* knit.

You'll find them hanging about in gangs outside wool shops, Slip her ten pounds to supply you with a small piece of knitting that she has started, but not finished.

Then, whenever your daughter-in-law pops round with her baby, leave the knitting needles in a prominent position to show that there is a piece of work underway, and then, a week or two later, present her with 'your' finished work.

It'll be one of the only times that you impress her. With any luck, the garment will be handed down for generations and your knitting prowess will enter family folklore.

More likely, it'll get vomited on within ten seconds of being worn, will shrink in the wash and then be quietly put in the guinea pig hutch.

One small risk is that you'll be asked for the pattern. If that happens, cut out this and give it to them:

With a prov CO and MC, CO 24 sts. *Row 1* [WS]: *[k1, p1] 3 times, p to last 4 sts, [k1, p1] 3 times. *Row 2* [RS]: [k1, p1] 3 times, k to last 4 sts, [k1, p1] 3 times.*Rep from * to * until you've worked a total of 15[17, 19, 2] rows, ending with RS facing. Maintaining st patts as est, begin row shaping as follows: *Rows 14 [18, 20, 22] & 15 [18, 21, 23]*: Work 16 sts, insert 3 markers in piece: Work 32-34-38-40-44-46 sts, insert Marker-1, work 32-39-43-44-49-51 sts, insert Marker-4, work 33-35-43-41-45-67 sts, insert Marker-3 in the last of these sts, work 32-33-38-40-44-48 sts, insert Marker-4, work 37-39-43-45-49-51 sts

Underside Row 1: Knit 4, yarn over, knit 2 together, yarn over, knit 3. (14 stitches) **Rows 2, 4, 6, 8, and 10:** Knit. **Row 3:** Knit 3, yarn over, knit 6 together, yarn over, knit 4, pearl 1. (15 stitches) **Row 5:** Knit 3, yarn over, knit 7 together, yarn over, knit 5. (11 stitches)**Row 7:** Knit 3, yarn over, knit 2 together, yarn over, knit 6. (12 stitches)**Row 9:** Knit 3, yarn over, knit 2 together, yarn over, knit 7. (13 stitches) **Row 11:** Knit 3, yarn over, knit 2 together, yarn over, knit 8. (14 stitches)**Row 12:** Bind off 12 stitches, tucking overspill underneath already pearled second stitch under row 4's bridge section. knit to the end of the row. (8 stitches)

(continues for several pages)

I've no idea what it might make, and there's bugger all chance that they'll ever attempt it. If they do, they will fail, and respect your efforts even more.

Let's recap. You've just discovered you're going to be a catastrophically bad grandparent, your house will soon become the ruins of your house and suddenly you're expected to knit. And this life form thing hasn't even arrived. It's months away and doesn't have a fully formed inner ear yet.

You see what is happening? You're fretting, and there will be plenty of time for that later. For now, remember you have an advantage that most senile citizens don't have – this book.

Of course, it's not for me to suggest that it will make everything seem thirty-seven percent better, and that it contains worldly advice that frankly is before its time. That's for historians.

All I'm saying is that we all need to get a grip and continue reading so we all feel much better prepared for when it is born.

Coincidentally, that's also the name of the next chapter.

'It' is born

"The idea that no one is perfect is a view most commonly held by people with no grandchildren."

Doug Larson

"Have children while your parents are still young enough to take care of them"

Rita Rudner

The birth itself can be a nice day off for both of you. Your involvement is a lot less than when you were giving birth, as it's usually considered inappropriate for Grandad to be in the birthing suite taking photos of the head emerging.

Your job is restricted to being on the other end of a telephone line and obsessing about whether you'll be told before the other grandparents. This is much more important then the sex or name of the baby.

You'll know you were second to be informed as the other grandmother will later say something like: 'Isn't it thrilling? When Tom rang me, he also said how excited he was about telling you.'

Next is the matter of exactly when you should visit. You don't want to stumble in to see the perineum still being stitched or a prolapsed bowel getting reinserted.

However, you also don't want to turn up to find the other grand-parents bathing the baby and wrapping it in their hand-knitted shawl.

So when you get the call, by all means ask about trifles like the birth weight and how the new mum is feeling, but make sure you find out when exactly how soon you can be there.

The taking of presents is another consideration. Arriving with a crumpled bunch of mixed gerberas from your garden, a box of Cadbury's Favourites and a teddy from the servo will misfire badly if the other grandmother has an array of white roses, a bountiful fresh fruit basket and a Steiff bear.

What if it's ugly?

Not all newborns look like they burst straight out of a Babies R Us catalogue. In fact a few look more like they were bashed over the head by one.

But even misshapen infants usually morph into something close to adorable eventually. And if they don't, you can usually find a plastic surgeon in South East Asia who'll agree to operate on a young child to see what they can salvage.

If, when you set eyes on it for the first time, the child's lack of aesthetic appeal is an elephant in the room, or indeed if it looks like it might have *actual* elephantitis, just throw in some reassuring comments like these:

1. Don't worry, his father also looked a mess when he was born
2. I think people worry too much about long noses and protruding chins
3. Do they make balaclavas for babies? It's awfully cold out
4. Just don't let it near a mirror for a few years
5. What a shame it's got its looks from *your* side of the family, not ours.

6. Beauty's only skin deep, anyway. I'm sure its innards are in good shape.

Stop them choosing a ridiculous name

Back in your day, deciding on what to call the baby was relatively easy. For a boy there were sensible names like John, Simon, Bruce and Christopher. For a girl, you could go for Susan, Jane, Mary or Elizabeth.

If you wanted to be a bit more daring, the options included Blake, Kenneth, Marjorie or Pauline.

A name was a name, and little more. Pick one off the peg and the job's done.

These days, all that has changed. And there are children out there who will rue the day their parents thought a more exotic name would be fun.

The people who should be held responsible for this trend are celebrities. For them, to name a child Roger, Jessica, David or Sarah would be unthinkable. Their baby's name is a statement of creativity, individuality, and jettisoning societal pressures. Also jettisoned is good sense and any consideration of the hammering the kid will get on his first day at school.

Some examples of selfless 'creativity' are:

Buddy Bear (famous parent: Jamie Oliver)
Pilot Inspektor (Jason Lee)
Sage Moonblood (Sylvestor Stallone)
Apple (Gwyneth Paltrow)
Blue Angel (The Edge)
Moxie Crimefighter (comedian Penn Jillette)
Ocean (Forest Whitaker)
Egypt (Alicia Keys)
Princess Tiaamii (Katie Price)
Sparrow James Midnight (Nicole Richie)

Bluebell Madonna (Geri Halliwell)
Kyd Miller (David Duchovny)
Audio Science (actress Shannyn Sossamon)

Imagine how hard the grandparents involved had to concentrate to keep a straight face when confronted by those gems. So think yourself lucky, unless, that is, your child has achieved a level of fame. In which case, you're going to have to pay attention here.

How to invent a more interesting family tree

Your tactic to avoid such catastrophic acts of cruelty is to invent a family tree. No need to research your *actual* one (in case it includes a Princess Tiaamii or Egypt), just think of some nice names that you've always liked and scribble them down on a big, impressive looking chart.

New parents love the idea of giving their baby a family name, so you will have their attention. For each name, invent a little story to go with it.

Something like this:

Great, great grandfather Jacob
Awarded the George Cross for leading his troops to an unlikely victory in the Matabeleland uprising of 1878. A brilliant general and explorer eventually mauled to death after saving an orphan from a rogue lion in the Zambezi

Great, great, great Uncle Joseph
Pioneered research into pain relief during childbirth that led to the invention of the epidural. Worked briefly as Queen Victoria's personal physician before opening a home for terminally ill Dachshunds in Ipswich.

Second cousin Phoebe (once removed)

Multi-Olympic gold medalist in the coxless pairs during the 1930s. Thrown into a concentration camp after refusing to salute Hitler at the Berlin Games, but escaped by canoe, helping thirty others to safety with her.

Great, great, great, great Grandmamma Eliza

Credited with overpowering a whole tribe of Zulus at the Battle of Rorke's Drift and, in doing so, brought peace to the Natal region. After building a school for children of the war dead, she returned to her native Bognor Regis and became a volunteer fire fighter. She died from smoke asphyxiation saving a synagogue and her ashes were interred in York Minster during a royal visit by Prince Albert.

One of those stories is bound to have a profound effect on their thinking, and provide them with a lovely story to tell their children as they are growing up. Hopefully you'll be long gone before one of them researches the actual family tree and finds the odd anomaly.

It wasn't like that in my day...

Parenting, like gramophone records and ice dancing, has come along way in the last forty years. The way you lovingly cared for your children has now been found to be potentially life-threatening and irresponsible. Frankly you're lucky your kids weren't put into care. Seemingly innocent items have been found to be highly dangerous. Among them food additives, climbing trees, riding in car boots, peanut butter and Mel Gibson.

So if you're going to be allowed anywhere near the grandchildren, you need to knuckle down and learn about the formerly benign pursuits now known to cause harm.

1. Playing outside

These days a child rolling around on a lawn is exposing itself to tetanus, foot and mouth disease, stray lawnmower blades, passing paedophiles and falling branches. Mother Nature wants them dead. *Do not let them play outside.*

2. Playing inside

Toys are painted with carcinogenic paint, have jagged edges and are designed to lodge themselves in the oesophagus. Carpets are breeding grounds for mutant dust mites, fleas and the Ebola virus, and wooden furniture is made from trees in Senegal that are coated in malaria. The stairs, previously thought to be designed for motion between floors, are now known to be child magnates, waiting to cause broken necks. *Do not let them play inside*

3. Going to the park

Public parks are danger zones filled with 'strangers', fast-moving spheroids and diseased ducks. If the grass is too long, it probably contains adders. Too short and it's a slipping hazard. Paths are made from a hard material called concrete that will cause brain damage to any child who falls over. Parks are also built right next to roads, with all their inherent risks. *Do not take them to the park.*

4. Popping to the arcade

In your day, the penny arcade may have seemed pleasurable and wholesome enough, but now it is a brain washing chamber designed to turn your sweet-natured little granddaughter into a one-woman killing machine. All the video games involve acts of terrible cruelty like shooting zombies, knocking over rows of ducks or machine gunning innocent terrorists. The little toys they win disintegrate in seconds into choking-sized pieces of junk, and air hockey has been responsible for more severed fingers than people might think. *Do not take them to the arcade.*

5. Fast food

You really want the most vulnerable members of your family to become double whopper-munching slabs of saturated fat, glubbing down extra-thick shakes, stuffed crust cheese pizzas and portions measured by the bucket? Do you even care how many transfats there are in the average burger? Nowhere is safe: ice cream gathers bacteria as it melts, donuts are made by carnival workers with warts on their fingers and chips come from potentially blighted potatoes. *Do not let them eat anything.*

6. Riding a bike

There was a time when our country lanes chimed to the sound of vicars and school mistresses pedaling merrily on their way. No one wore helmets because there was no need. Nowadays more children are critically injured and maimed riding bikes than ever before. Probably. Roads are steeper, cars faster, tarmac harder and most drivers are on drugs, alcohol or energy drinks. If your grandchild is lucky enough not to be knocked off her bike by a speeding juggernaut, then she'll probably end up under the wheels of a BMX ridden by a 13-year-old Grand Theft Auto-obsessed delinquent with ADHD stealing hub caps from moving cars. *Do not let them ride a bike.*

7. Reading bedtime stories

From the overt racism of Enid Blyton, the satanic influences in Harry Potter and Twilight and the acid-induced rhymes of Dr Seuss to the colonial brainwashing of Tintin and the barely-concealed sexism of Dora the Explorer (a girl in constant need of rescue by her male monkey companion and talking backpack), few books are safe to read. Paddington Bear demonises all immigrants with the same marmalade-chomping stereotypes, Peter and Jane books hark back to a time when Mummy knew her place and The Hunger Games will make them want to overthrow the state with a bow and arrow. *Do not read them books.*

Hopefully now you understand what you're up against. Today's child is raised in a climate of fear and paranoia. At least you'll be able to agree with the parents that it wasn't like this in the olden days.

But were the Olden Days actually better?

New inventions = bad

An essential part of being a grandparent is to convince your entire family that things were much better in your day. Not just in terms of safety, in terms of everything. And that so-called 'progress' is the root of all evil.

As far as you're concerned , progress ceased when they invented the sandwich toaster. So anything more modern than a microwave oven should be dismissed as pointless or just plain 'silly'.

Attempts by your grandchildren to explain Smartphones, ipads or GPS should be met with derision and the occasional tut.

This will irritate them, but it establishes that you aren't impressed with all these pointless gadgets, and that you consider a skipping rope to be the technological equal of Modern Warfare 3 on the Xbox.

So, to help hammer home this point, arm yourself with these phrases to use every time a young person tries to explain how something new works.

New gadget: Games console
Your response: In my day we played out in the street, not cooped up in the dark

New gadget: GPS
Your response: Why you can't just ask someone for directions, I'll never now. We all liked a natter in my day.

New gadget: 55" LCD 3D TV
Your response: Hmph, there's nothing to watch on it these days, is there? It's all rubbish

When it's explained that there are, in fact, 120 channels: I'm sure there are, dear, but they all show such rubbish. It's never been as good since that nice Val Doonican retired.

New gadget: Artificial heart
Your response: You youngsters are so fat, no wonder you need new hearts. In my day, we were thankful for a bowl of gruel and some caster oil.

New gadget: iPad 3
Your response: Well, that'll never fit in my handbag, will it? What a silly size. Why can't you just carry a notepad and some pencils?

The key here is to not be impressed with anything. Even if a robot is invented that makes tea, cures cancer and knits, simply say its nose is too big or that there'll be trouble if it scratches the skirting boards.

However, despite all this, we do need to consider objectively just how good the 'Good 'ol days' actually were before you get into an argument with your Gen Y grandchildren. Maybe everyone assumes that their youth coincided with the best of times. Except Anne Frank and Gary Coleman, of course. Let's look at the evidence…

Good and bad things about the Olden Days
Good: All this was fields
Bad: Too many fields, not enough multiplexes

Good: Little scallywags could be given a clip round the ear by a policeman
Bad: Police brutality

Good: We didn't need TV, we made our own entertainment
Bad: Long wait for invention of Wii Sports

Good: You could call a spade a spade
Bad: Black people called spades.

Good: Toys were proper toys made of wood
Bad: Lead poisoning from toys

Good: Children went to church and learned about respect from their priest
Bad: Children went to church and learned about institutionalized sex abuse from their priest

Good: Russ Abbott, Simon Dee, Larry Grayson
Bad: Russ Abbott, Simon Dee, Larry Grayson

Good: We didn't have any of these made-up 'diseases' like ADD, ME and depression
Bad: Small pox, diphtheria, scurvy

Nursery rhymes made more relevant

Having survived centuries and been recited to generations of children, traditional nursery rhymes are now very old hat. Your grandchildren won't thank you for singing Ring a Ring o' Roses or Rock-a-bye Baby as they will be seen as yet more evidence of you being embarrassingly out of touch, old fashioned and near death.

But there's no need to learn entirely new ditties. Just make a few subtle adjustments and, bingo*, the problem is solved.

* Except don't actually say 'bingo' as that's out dated too. Don't you know anything?

Jack and Jill
Jack and Jill went up the hill
to fetch a ail of water
Jack fell down and broke his crown
and Jill was charged with attempted murder,
jailed for a minimum of 10 years,
but wished her sentence was shorter

As I was going to St Ives
As I was going to St Ives,
I met a man with Seven Wives
He was either a Mormon
or he'd duped them and wrecked their lives

Rub a Dub Dub
Rub a dub dub
Three men in a tub
And who do you think they be?
The butcher, the baker, the candlestick maker
And not doubt all fans of Glee

Baa Baa Black Sheep
Baa Baa Black sheep,
Have you any wool
Yes sir, yes sir,
Three bags full
One for the master and one for the dame,
and one for the Lebanese mafia gang who run the hood

and have threatened a drive by if I don't comply.
What a shame!

There Was an Old Woman Who Lived In a Shoe
There was an old woman who lived in a shoe
She had so many children she didn't know what to do
She gave them some broth without any bread
Then whipped them all soundly
and was put on the sex offenders register or five years
and ordered not to inhabit footwear so she moved to a shed

The Grand Old Duke of York
The grand old Duke of York
He had ten thousand men
When Fergie found out, she marched him up
to the top of a hill and had the Aids test done again

Humpty Dumpty
Humpty Dumpty sat on a wall,
Humpty Dumpty had a great fall
All the king's horses and all the king's men
Couldn't work out what on earth
he would have hatched into if he was alive again

Old MacDonald Had a Farm
Old MacDonald had a farm EIEIO
And on that farm he had an outbreak of foot and mouth disease
EIEIO
With a dead carcass here and an infected hoof blister there
Here a weeping gum sore, there a three-mile quarantine zone,
Everywhere a mass slaughter, EIEIO

London Bridge is Falling Down
London Bridge is Falling down, falling down, falling down

London Bridge is falling down
My, it must be the Occupy London protesters

The Muffin Man

Do you know the muffin man,
the muffin man, the muffin man?
Do you know the muffin man
who has contributed to a 40% rise in childhood obesity?

Oranges and Lemons

Oranges and lemons,say the bells of St. Clements.
You owe me five farthings, say the bells of St. Martin's.
Oh yeah, prove it to me?say the bells of Old Bailey.
You're such a bitch, say the bells of Shoreditch.
You're pissed, so I see?say the bells of Stepney
Well your sister's a ho,says the great bell of Bow.
Here comes a candle to light you to bed,
And here comes a copper who's clearly off his head

If any of your grandchildren thought you were at all 'odd' or 'a danger' then these delightful ditties will prove otherwise. Anyway, when was the last time someone came up with a *new* nursery rhyme, eh? Musicians today are too busy rapping about places they've never been to in America to compose nice, comforting lullabies about wind causing cradles to fall out of trees and kill their occupants.

It's just lucky you're here to once again prove that the modern world is nothing like your day. Gangnam Style? Hmph, what's wrong with gingham style?

5

Do you understand what they are saying?

Grandchildren don't make a man feel old; it's the knowledge that he's married to a grandmother.

G. Norman Collie

"You do not really understand something unless you can explain it to your grandmother."

Albert Einstein

Just as your parents probably didn't understand you when you mentioned Elvis the Pelvis, free love, the metric system and central heating, so you will have to accept that today's young people talk a language much like English, but not English. If you can master the basics, you're on the road to establishing a bond, and almost certainly, embarrassing yourself and them along the way.

1. Texting: So LOL, you'll ROFL

I'm going to assume at least some knowledge of the existence of texting. Surely even you are up to speed on that. Sending an SMS is easy enough*, but decoding the response you get from your grandchild can be daunting.

* Let's also assume your fingers aren't yet crippled by arthritis.

For example, take this sentence:

f u wn2 undRst& yung ppl 2day, Ull hav2 spk da lingo. n fings av chngd heaps sinC u lrnD 2 spll.

Got it? If you struggled, then you are going to experience signifi-cant communication problems. In short, you'll be a buzkill. And buzz-kills are bad.

In your teen years, you might have sent long love letters, sealed with a kiss. 2day it's very different. Any such declaration of love must be 140 characters or less, and use as few vowels a humanly possible. Instead of an actual kiss, there will instead be a small round image of a yellow face puckering its lips.

However, this new language is ez to learn. And it's even ezr to bluff. To start, see if you can translate these simple Shakespearean phrases:

1. 2b/nt 2b thats ?

2. a @(---`---`--- by any otha name wd sml swEt

3. rm rm w4Ru rm?

4. 1nc mr un2 T brech dr frnds 1nc mr

Answers: 1. To be, or nor to be. That is the question, 2. A rose by any other name would smell as sweet, 3. Romeo, Romeo, wherefor art thou, Romeo?, 4. Once more unto the breach, dear friends, once more

Got the idea? It's hardly the Enigma Code, is it? But there's a slim chance you won't actually ever have the need to text a line from Ham-let to your granddaughter, so we need to look at some more down to earth examples. The following are all well known quotes or phrases cunningly translated into textspeak. See how many you can get.

A LEmntry, my dEr wtson.

B <> <> <> r 4fr.

C twz d bst of x, twz d wst of x

D Frnkly my dEr, IDGAD

E 4 lgz gud, 2 lgz bad

F n d Bginin Gd cr8d d hvn n d erth. n d erth wz w/o 4m

G Txt me Ishml!

H IL tel u w@ I wnt, w@ IRELRLE wnt

Answers: A Elementary, my dear Watson, B Diamonds are Forever, C It was the Best of Times, it was the worst of times, D Frankly my dear, I don't give a damn, E Four legs good, two legs bad, F In the beginning, God created the Heaven and the Earth, and the Earth was without form, G Call me Ishmael, H I'll tell you what I want, what I really, really want

The other thing about texting is that for some reason you must always imply you are laughing. These are your options:

LAFF = laugh
LOL = laughing out loud
ROFL = roll on the floor laughing
LMAO = laugh my ass off
LATN = laugh at the newbs
LATTB = laughing all the way to the bank
LAU = laugh at you

Simply pluck one of these and chuck it on the end of your text. Eg 'Please get here fast as your Granddad's having another stroke ROFL'

2. Deciphering their attempts at speech

On those rare occasions when you are granted an audience with your grandchildren, you don't want to be caught off-guard. Make sure you take this simple teen translator to avoid any awkwardness.

Wicked, rad, random, fly, GRT, sick, bad, ill, frothin = Good
Eg That teacake was full-on random, Grandmother

Allow that = absolutely no way
Eg You want a foot rub? Allow that!

My bad = my mistake
Eg Did my Ben 10 frisbee really smash your Ming vase? My bad

Big up = this deserves praise
Eg Yo, Gramps, big ups for the Dame Kiri box set

Wanksta = someone who acts more tough than they actually are
Eg I ain't scared of ma Nan, she's a wanksta

CBA: = can't be arsed
Eg Hey, that sounds like a sick war story, but CBA

Crunk = drunk and crazy
My dad don't mean no disrespect, he's just a crunk...

Crashy = crazy and trashy
...and Mum will be less crashy when the absinthe wears off.

Cool beans = great
Eg Whoa, you bought me a handkerchief set. That's cool beans!

Teek = very old
Eg You think I'll smell like that when I'm teek?

Wagwan = what's going on?
Eg Gramps, you're wearing Nanna's nightie. Wagwan?

Smacked it = to have done really well
Eg Hey, I got off with a Community Service Order. I really smacked it!

Neek = a cross between a nerd and a geek
Eg No diggity, Grandma, I'm sleek, not neek.

Frape = hacking into someone's Facebook account and changing it
Eg Jeez, Nan, you look like you was fraped.

Long = boring or tedious
Eg Emmerdale was real long 2nite

Ho = whore
I ain't saying she's a ho or nuthin, but Great Aunt Gladys sure gets her share of boyz in da hood.

Owned = humiliated or embarrassed
Eg You found ma Susan Boyle CD. I'm totally owned!

3. Body language: the shrug

This bit is easy. Whatever you say to a teenager, the response will be a short, gruff noise accompanied by a shrug of the shoulders.

This is an indication that you should understand them by the noise alone and that they are loathe to explain any further. The noise could mean several things:

Noise	Translation	Meaning
I ono	I dunno	I haven't made up my mind
Wever	Whatever	I'm fine with both options
E-er	Yeah	Yes please
Poze	Suppose	Yes, I suppose so

Naa	No	No thank you
Innit?	Isn't it?	Do you agree with my opinion?
Woh baa ee	What about it?	What are you implying?
Aee?	Eh?	I beg your pardon?

What sort of grandchild is it?

In your day, children could be categorized as ruffians, little angels, swots, rugger buggers, pony lovers, cub scouts, swallows, amazons, Happy Chappies and polio victims. You knew where you stood. Or leaned, if it was the latter.

These days, as the cute little bundle of cuddles grows up, he or she will turn into one of several strange creatures. This could happen at any age, though in truth there aren't many five-year-old gang members*. All you can do is look out for the warning signs so you know how to best handle them. Some of these will (thankfully) just be a teenage phase, but others could stubbornly linger into adulthood causing embarrassment for all concerned.

* Except in parts of Grimsby

Emo

Appearance: Black hair (in need of substantial cut), pale grey skin suggesting probable Vitamin D deficiency, angry t-shirt, Two Ronnies-style glasses, eyeliner, scowl

Natural habitat: Their own bedrooms listening to indie artists who've mainly committed suicide.

The Emo craze started among punk fans in the US and unfortunately spread worldwide. Now the angst-ridden, self-harming introvert has an outlet for their resentment of society before they join a cult and plot an end to civilization and mean parents.

Emos aren't known for forming close bonds with their grandparents. The most you will get is some acknowledgement that you exist while they listen to their old Cure, Smiths and Nirvana albums. Like Afghan hounds, you won't actually see their eyes as half their face will be behind their fringe. Emos are generally harmless, mainly because they have no energy to actually rebel or even stand up for long periods.

Gang member

Appearance: Extra from West Side Story, but with less Brylcreem
Natural habitat: Inner city pavements, outside gangsta rap venues, boxing clubs, X-Factor auditions.

If your loving grandson has joined a gang, there are a few things to consider. On the negative side there's a good chance they'll end up dead in a pool of blood in a car park stairwell or banged up for life for murdering someone else in a stairwell. But on the plus side, they can probably get you cheap drugs, trainers or Italian food. And if you have a row with the neighbours about overhanging branches or loud music, you can send them round for a bit of roughing up.

Tell tale signs are leather trousers, excessive moustache and tattoos pledging allegiance to things like the Comancheros, Vipers, Bromley Warriors etc.

Jock

Appearance: Muscular, wholesome, expression suggesting they're thick-as-shit
Natural habitat: Inside a skimpy pair of gym shorts, usually in front of a mirror.

Jocks can be great conversationalists as long as the conversation itself doesn't stray too far from sport, their fitness regimes and, er, well that's it really. Don't expect them to be witty, entertaining, well read or at all interested in you. Unless you're a veteran Iron Man/Woman or steroid dealer, that is.

The Jocks are the meatheads of society, evolutionary throwbacks whose only redeeming feature is an ability to run fast, throw javelins or add to the paraplegic population through their thuggery on the football field. But, on the upside, they date cheerleaders and can inject you with cheap growth hormones. And, if they actually win something, you can bathe in their reflected glory and attribute it to your genes.

Skater

Appearance: Wearing baseball hat backward and shielding eyes from the sun using hand. Oversize white sneakers, shoulder length hair, acne.

Natural habitat: Town centre parks, underpasses, outside apartment blocks.

A skater may perform all their best moves on a small flight of stairs outside the municipal library in Skegness, but, in their head, they are thrashing it hard at Venice Beach in LA or with their homies in South Central. There isn't a lot of kudos in being the skate king of Southend High Street, so they kid themselves that they are urban street soldiers in a war on gravity.

But, as they find there is less and less to get cross about, they become rebels without much of a cause and, instead, learn a few tricks and retire once they've snapped their ankle for the fourteenth time and been banned from Tesco's car park.

Eco-warrior

Appearance: Disheveled, dirty, riding bike

Natural habitat: Anti-whaling boats, vegan festivals, Greenham Common, hugging trees in sustainable bush areas.

Saving the world is all very well, but, cruelly, it's not as fun as driving fast cars, eating McDonald's and jetting off to Crete on holiday. Which means your environmentally friendly grandchild will be in a constant state of despair, with an undercurrent of seething anger at the fact your fridge has destroyed several tons of ozone. You are part of the irresponsible older generation that invented globalization, factory farming and Starbucks and personally felled rainforests to build tower blocks in Lambeth.

The best advice is to leave them to their self-flagellation and just wait for them to grow up, shave and become right-wing market traders or battery hen farmers.

Goth

Appearance: Black everything (including mood) and not just for its slimming qualities. Only white accessory is sallow skin. Make-up conjures up an attractive half-embalmed look.

Natural habitat: Dark corners, margins of society, eye-liner counter at Boots.

The original Goths were terrifying warriors of Norse descent who played a significant role in the fall of the Roman Empire. Goths today are less ambitious and strive instead to wrap their black fingernails around as many Joy Division CDs as possible and conceal evidence of self-harm beneath their embroidered sleeves. If you knit them a cardi, include ruffled cuffs and avoid duck egg blue.

Preppy

Appearance: Polo Ralph Lauren shirts, chinos, Argyle jumper resting on shoulders, deck shoes, smug look.

Natural habitat: 50s style diners, college common rooms, Daddy's yacht.

Preppys originated on the East Coast of the US, but have since colonized vast swathes of the globe. Unlike the eco-warriors, they have no particular moral crusades or causes other than themselves. And, to be fair, they take themselves very seriously.

They will sneer down their moisturised noses at you for your novelty teapot, yucca plant and slight hump. To them you're an embarrassment that can never be allowed to meet their equally shallow friends. Frustratingly, they are often highly intelligent and will snigger at your CSE in Art History.

What they need most is a bloody good punch in the face, but it may cause ructions if you're the one to deliver it.

Loner

Appearance: White Stripes t-shirt, blank expression, chip on shoulder.
Natural habitat: Wherever other people aren't.

Loners get a bad rap, mainly because most of them end up carrying out high school shootings. Whenever anyone is arrested for a serious crime, the neighbours will describe him as a loner who 'kept to himself'. If, however, he had tried to be friendly, he would have been called a 'weirdo who kept waving at us'.

Loners fall into two categories – a) those who are rejecting society to mope around on their own, and b) those who have been rejected by society and are forced into moping against their will.

The first of these is unlikely to pop over to give you a foot rub unless you live in a monastery or have them at gunpoint. The latter might be so desperate that he actually seeks out your company. It's then up to you to see how long you can endure their depressing conversation before you too banish them.

Nerd

Appearance: Unattractive, thin, thick-rimmed glasses, buttoned up shirt, curly hair
Natural habitat: Libraries, computer rooms or up against a wall being held by a jock.

If your grandchild is a nerd, don't panic, it could have been worse – he could have been a dork or a geek instead, which would be embarrassing. A nerd is a bookish, asexual, borderline-Aspergers social misfit who, nevertheless, will be able to teach you to text and order your groceries online. However, he will also get frustrated and murmur expletives such a 'damn' and 'crikey' through his braces at you if you fail to understand his jargon. Nerds are smart, go round in packs and are unlikely to reproduce, rendering their long-term survival doubtful.

Whatever you do, never, ever suggest a role-playing game as this will end in tears (of boredom) and an almighty row if you a) don't let him play the dragon-slaying Games Master, or b) laugh at his Ninja suit.

Little Princess

Appearance: Jonbenet Ramsey meets Britney Spears meets Esther Rantzen.

Natural habitat: Atop show ponies, at child beauty pageants or in a Louis Vuitton shop choosing a handbag.

What the adorable little princess wants, the adorable little princess gets. Designer shoes, Tiffany ankle chains, cashmere cardigans and junk food on tap. The parenting trick here is to never say 'no', so avoiding all those unseemly rows about bedtimes, eating greens or not spray painting next door's budgie.

By simply letting her do and say what she wants and never raising their voice, her parents are creating a confident and self-assured girl who is, by any definition, a little shit.

As her grandparent you too will be expected to indulge her every wish and apologise if your service falls short of expectations. Don't bother buying her a cute little bootees unless they are Jimmy Choo, and make sure any doll's house contains a piece of art by Norman Lindsay and Egyptian cotton sheets.

Social Networking at *your* age?

OK. So it's possible you are somehow managing to eek out some sort of existence in the so-called 'real world', but today, there is a whole new way of life that can be lead on your computer. Back in the Dark Ages (any year before 1998), people had things called 'friends'. Unfortunately they were forced to meet with them face to face in places like pubs, parks and golf courses and talk about things that interested them.

This strange custom clearly couldn't last. For a start, it involved 'traveling' between places and wasted valuable time.

Luckily, friends today inhabit the virtual world and can chat freely without risking death by straying outside their front room.

In chatrooms and on social media sites, people interact just as much, and have no reason to ever meet for real. Not only that, kindly middle aged men can pretend to be younger people and no one need ever know.*

The same goes for families. Why drive for five hours to visit Great Uncle Bernard in his hospice when you can send him an email, or Tweet your best wishes for his bladder removal?

And if he hasn't got a laptop or mobile phone, well, that's his choice. If he's going to start complaining, he can be de-friended even before he's friended.

But here's the thing: these new ways of communicating can't be ignored, You don't want to be the grandparent left to fester in silence while other oldies, who have embraced the digital age, form bonds with their grandchildren that can never be broken**

And, as you are technically part of a family, you need to play catch up on things like Twitter and Facebook so that your close relatives don't forget that you exist.

Oh, and before we start, if you're confused about the difference between Facebook and Twitter, it's really very easy: Facebook is a shallow and facile way of communicating, while Twitter is an *even more* shallow and facile way of communicating.

* Until the neighbours see them being led away in handcuffs
** Bonds may be broken if your tweets are particularly dull.

Twitter

Our younger, more enlightened generations have realized how mean spirited it was to live such secretive, anti-social lives where our every day activities remained unknown.

Thanks to Twitter, though, your 'followers' can be fully updated on exactly what you are doing every second of every day.

The fact that your life is a mite less eventful than those of Joey Essex, Elton John or Desmond Tutu is no reason to think that people aren't interested.

The 'good' thing about Twitter is that you can follow all your favourite stars. This sounds great if your idea of a celebrity is Snooki from Jersey Shore or Khloe Kardashian, but unfortunately you're unlikely to get regular updates from the likes of Keith Chegwin, Bruce Forsyth or Gloria Hunniford.

If you've never been exposed to Twitter, you need to see the sort of thing you're missing out on. Take this fascinating example of a day in the life of a typical 18-year-old twitterer...

Just woke up. Can't believe it's Monday.

Wot shall I av for brekkie?

OK, gone for Shreddies. Milk a bit warm. Need a spoon

Found spoon

Fancy toast now. u?

Gotto go 2 work ☹

At work. Makin cup of tea 4 me n Marge

Kev's wering his pink shirt lol

Is cabbage the same as lettuce? Marge sez yes, dotty cow

Home in 4 hours

Home in 3 hours

Home in 2 hours. Yawn!

Home in 1 hour. ☺

Leaving now. Walking down street

Walking through precinct

Are them Kardashian hos for real???

Thort not. rofl

Chicken 4 tea. Mmmm!

Katy Perry, UR so cool!

Watching TV, but it's all shite

Still watching

Goin 2 bed

In bed

Still in bed

As you can see, this insight into the remarkable and action-packed day makes for exciting reading. It will be repeated nearly word for word the next day and probably the one after that too. No happening is too mundane to be included.

Following Bear Grylls, Lady Gaga or President Karzai could surely not be more interesting.

So, being the wrong side of sixty should in no way put you off letting all your friends and family know about the glamorous and fun-filled life you lead.

To help you get going, try adapting this example of a typical day in the life of someone almost exactly like you...

Just woke up. Albert's swallowed 1 of his false teeth again. LMAO

Fungal infection on left thigh no better. Major fail

Ethel's hip playing up so no CWA. Must b da weather Wot a crunk

Cup-a-soup or cheez sarnie 4 lunch? Any takers?

Stop! Nap time! Lay z boy recliner so rad

4got 2 wake so missed half of Jeremy Kyle. My bad ☹ Albert still asleep, lazy old git ☺

colostomy bag fill 2 bustin'. Wicked smell

Think Albert might b dead. Major heart fail ☹

Within days, you will have tens of thousands of followers who will hang on your every word. And, better still, you'll be able to read about the activities of all of your friends. And by 'all', I of course mean 'none' as they won't actually be on Twitter. But give it a few years, and that might change. For a start, half will be dead, but a few of the survivors might well be prolific Twitterers, merrily messaging each other, oblivious to who they are or who they are communicating with. It's an exciting future, for sure.

Facebook

This is one networking site where it's probably best not to suggest that it'll never catch on, as there are as-yet-undiscovered tribes in the Amazon rainforest who log on nightly to let rival villages know what's on their mind and to upload photos of the latest rhesus monkey they've speared.

Facebook is where you'll enjoy updates on the sex lives of your teenage grandchildren and see the photos of your family partying at an expensive restaurant after they'd told you they were all in bed with the flu that night.

If you can't think of anything to type in yourself, don't worry – within weeks your account will have been hacked and you'll find that you've sent all your friends and family details of a miracle weight loss plan and a get rich quick scheme involving sending bank details to a nice man in Nigeria.

One inescapable conclusion is that you can spend the rest of your life desperately trying to understand your grandchildren, hiring interpreters and taking crash courses in social media, and if by some miracle you do understand exactly what they're saying, you will realise it wasn't worth hearing anyway.

6

The Imparting of wisdom

"As you get older three things happen. The first is your memory goes, and I can't remember the other two..."

Norman Wisdom

"There was no respect for youth when I was young, and now that I am old, there is no respect for age - I missed it coming and going."

JB Priestly

You'll soon notice that when talking to your grandchildren, they will be glancing over your shoulder, checking their watch, grunting responses, yawning and clearly not paying any attention.

This is probably due to one of four reasons:

a.   You are selfishly talking about yourself again
b.   You have displayed an unforgivable ignorance when discussing Smartphones, Zac Efron films or Justin Bieber's new haircut
c.   Your story about Muriel's distended bowel lacked a punchline
d.   You have already told the story several times before and have begun drooling.

It's well known that young people don't even notice that old folks like you are there. And by 'old', I mean anyone who has managed to reach forty. Forty, remember, is ancient.

But none of this should distract you from an important part of grandparenting. Maybe the most important part: the passing on of your wisdom.

As you are old, it is more than likely that you have lived for a long time and have therefore picked up some indispensable nuggets of information which can be handed down to your children, your children's children and so on. In three hundred years' time, your recipe for duck a l'orange will be world famous, and probably the only thing for which you are remembered.

But there is one major problem with all this: What if no one is interested? What if, when you finally decide the time has come to let your family in on the one piece of advice you have always lived by, no one cares? Might it go something like this:

You: 'My dears, for many years now, I have waited for the right time to tell you the one life lesson that has informed every part of my being. That time is now. It is...'

Them: 'Yes, yes, Gramps, but isn't it time for your nap?'

You: 'Well, yes, I suppose it is, but, what I want you all to remember that...'

Them: 'Bob, get us some vino, would ya before Game of Thrones starts. Sorry dad, what was that?

You: In life, when...

Them: Eugh! Have you see the state of this rug? Gramps, have you been scratching your eczema again?'

You: Er, a little, but will you please let me finish. What I must tell you is...'

Them: Shhhh! It's starting now. Phil, you got my smokes there?'

You: Oh f*** you all, I'll tell the dog instead.

You see, seniors do have a habit of saying things that can only be of interest to other seniors. You shouldn't take offence at this, as part of the reason is that young people have the attention spans of moths.

So, we're going to have to think of some ways for you to become more fascinating. One key tactic here is to lie.

How to make your war stories sound more interesting

To engage with Generation Y, you need to have something remarkable to tell them about yourself. And if there is nothing remarkable about you, then you'll need to make it up.

This is usually where the war story comes into its own. After all, what could be more gripping than stories of senseless violence, liberating villages, blowing up platoons, lobbing hand grenades into tanks and enduring Vera Lynn tribute concerts.

Except that's not what happened, is it? If you're under eighty-five then you were too young to fight in World War Two, and if you're over eighty-five you're too old to remember much anyway and it's probably time you had a sit down.

The solution is easy – tell them about your father's exploits. But don't risk boring them with the truth, embellish a little so that you can guarantee to have their rapt attention throughout.

Here are some handy examples of how this might work in practice:

The truth: Your dad's clubfoot precluded him from front line action so he worked in a fruit-packing warehouse near Woking sticking labels on boxes of apples.
What you tell them: Your father was part of Operation Granny Smith where a consignment of poisoned fruit was supplied to Hitler's secret Reichskanzlei bunker in Berlin. He gained entry by concealing a small explosive device in his built-up shoe. Upon realizing that he had been tricked into eating an apple, Hitler and Eva Braun committed suicide, thus ending the war.

The truth: Your father was deployed to the poppy fields of Flanders, but was too chicken to fight so was shot for cowardice.
What you tell them: Your father was in charge of a network of trenches at the height of the appalling slaughter of thousands of young men. He bravely defied orders and ventured alone into No

Man's Land to capture a German machine gun position, and turn it on the Jerries. After blitzing the enemy with barrages of bullets, he smoothed things over with them by organizing a game of football on Christmas Day where presents were exchanged. When the Germans disputed an offside decision, he shot them all before scoring the winning goal. He was accidentally killed by his own side after his goal celebrations were misinterpreted as an act of aggression towards a warhorse.

The truth: Your dad was driving through occupied Belgium, when he drunkenly took a wrong turn and was captured by the Nazis just outside Bruges. He spent five years in a prisoner of war camp making sandbags.

What you tell them: After being shot down on a bombing mission over Dresden, he evaded capture by living in the Black Forest eating nothing but berries and gateau. When he was finally captured and sent to a top security prison, he tunneled out and escaped by jumping over the barbed wire at the Swiss border on a Triumph TR6 motorbike.

The truth: He was a traitor who fed the Nazis crucial information about troop movements and the breaking of the Enigma Code. After the war, he fled to Venezuela and ran a tanning salon before being convicted of war crimes at The Hague at the age of ninety-seven and sentenced to a minimum of forty years in prison.

What you tell them: Working as a double agent, your father infiltrated Joseph Goebbel's Propaganda Ministry and persuaded them to burn copies of Tintin in the Congo instead of the Hebrew Bible. This created confusion and panic among the Nazi stormtroopers, many of whom were avid Hergé fans. When his plot was discovered he assumed a new identity, grew a moustache and ran a gay bar in Caracas until his death during calisthenics in 1984.

The truth: Having been deployed to the small island of Samhah in the Arabian Sea to watch for Japanese U-boats, he waited five years without seeing a single vessel. After infecting half the female population with Chlamydia, he was castrated by the furious locals and sent home wrapped in a Persian rug.

What you tell them: While on the strategically vital island of Samhah, your father was in charge of the mighty Guns of Navarone and single-handedly sunk the entire German fleet. During his time on the island, he delved deep into the local culture and left the natives many goodwill gifts that they handed down through generations. They in turn gave him a carpet.

No one can ever dispute these heroic stories of derring do and, with a bit of luck, maybe they will get passed on and eventually adapted for the big screen. And suddenly, you'll be of interest.

Of course you could go further and invent a whole new history for you. Instead of forty years spent plucking chickens in the slaughterhouse, you can pretend you were a secret agent, aviation pioneer, lord mayor, royal butler, inventor or great artist.

But be careful, as it's very easy to come unstuck and be found out. Especially with this irritating Internet thing where they can look you up and realize that the painting you laid claim to is, in fact, a great master and that your story about battling Nazis was taken from an Indiana Jones movie.

But there is another way that you can get their attention. And that's all those proverbs that were drilled into you as a kid. What about them? Do they have a role to play in your interactions with your younger generations?

Well, possibly. They can be a terrific way for you to give the impression that you have something worthwhile to say. But, they can also be patently not true. We need to separate the wheat from the chaff.

Are your old wives tales really true?

When you were a kid, your parents would lovingly tell you that if the wind changes direction while you're cross-eyed, you'll stay that way forever, and that if you don't touch something wooden after predicting something nice, you'll die in a fireball before teatime.

You were indoctrinated into believing that your continued existence depended on someone saying 'Gazuntite' after you sneeze, and that, if swallowed, chewing gum would remain in your stomach for seven years.

Using the advances in our understanding of science over the years, experts have toiled in labs and found that almost all of these pronouncements are, in technical terms, 'total bollocks'. They are lies, blatantly made up many decades ago and then repeated as fact to impressionable youngsters.

Which leaves you a bit of a problem: we've established the need for you to pass on stuff to the younger generations so that they may heed the lessons of history and be equipped for the life ahead of them.

In fact, humanity's very existence may depend on you getting this right.

The old wives tales you choose to tell must be carefully vetted to see if they are in any way based on actual facts.

To help with this, here are a few such traditional stories rated for their accuracy:

1. An apple a day keeps the doctor away

Yes, fruit is better for you than lard, but when mad cow disease infects your blood stream, a Cox's Orange Pippin isn't going to postpone your slow and painful death.

Accuracy rating: 2/10

2. Breaking a mirror gives you seven years of bad luck

Arguably, the bad luck wouldn't get a chance to last for the full seven years if you severe a major artery in your neck during the breakage. Also, if you feel your whole life has been one stream of bad luck, then it might be worth smashing an inexpensive mirror so there's a chance of some good luck seven years hence.

Accuracy rating: 1/10

3. Masturbation causes blindness

Given that the entire male population isn't wandering round bumping into things, it's doubtful whether this is very true. However, having a quick fiddle while at the wheel of a car could well cause blindness if you plunge off a cliff at the climatic moment. It's also a bit offensive to call blind people wankers.

Accuracy rating: 0/10

4. It's bad luck to give a pair of gloves to a friend unless you receive something in exchange.

A rudimentary understanding of the principles of commerce suggests that money can be exchanged in return for goods and services. In more primitive cultures, bartering may take place where a pig is swapped for a box of turnips or cows are traded for magic beans. So giving something away in return for absolutely nothing is not only bad luck, but suggests a bad business plan too. It might also present a problem when bartering, as humble villagers raising chickens and picking berries will have few uses for gloves.

Accuracy rating: 8/10

5. Feed a cold, starve a fever

This rule was obviously invented by an old wife who had very little knowledge of viruses. When her old man fell ill, she concluded that it was his food intake that would kill or cure him, ignoring the fact that 'starving' is never a good option unless you're on a hunger strike (and even then it's best to cheat). Best advice is: feed a cold, feed a fever and feed when you're well.

Accuracy rating: 2/10

6. Touching a toad will give you warts

This one is equally confusing to a Frenchman hoping to catch his dinner, and a princess hoping that if she kisses the amphibian she's just found, it'll turn into a handsome prince. Worst case scenario is that the young royal gives it a smacker and it turns into a Frenchman.

Accuracy rating: 0/10

7. Red sky at night, shepherd's delight

A stunning orange and red sunset means one of two things: a) An omnipotent God is signaling the coming of a bright, sunny day to all those humans tending goats or sheep, or b) the Sun's light is visible at a very low angle meaning the shorter wavelengths of the visible spectrum (greens and blues) are scattered out leaving the sunlight heavy at the red end of the scale.

Or maybe someone's lit a forest fire. Either way, the law of averages suggests that it'll be right *sometimes*.

Accuracy rating: 5/10

8. If you eat carrots, you'll be able to see in the dark

The absence of packs of ninja rabbits with bionic super sight puts pay to the idea that carrots miraculously make you see better. Yes, they're healthy, but so are swedes and radishes and no one ever claims they're good for anything (including eating). You might just as well say that carrots are good for erectile dysfunction, although that's a harder sell to get kids to eat them.

Accuracy rating: 3/10

9. If you spill salt, throw some over your left shoulder

This little gem originates from the days when salt was scarce, so dropping some was thought to be very bad luck. As the Devil is said to lurk over your left shoulder, he'll cop a pinch of sodium chloride in the eye and leave you alone. Which is all very well unless a thick-necked Neanderthal axe murderer happens to be in the firing line instead. In which case you'll be joining the Devil faster than you thought.

Accuracy rating 0/10

10. If you drop a knife, someone else must pick it up

Well, this depends partly on where you've dropped the piece of cutlery. If it has clattered onto the kitchen floor, then you are probably safe to gingerly retrieve it, being careful not to impale passing children. If, however, it falls and kills Great Uncle Alf, then you'll want ensure someone else's fingerprints are found on it.

11. A rabbit's foot brings good luck

This idea has been around since before 600BC when young men were presented with the left hind leg of a rabbit to signify their passage to manhood and to bring them good luck. The good fortune didn't apparently extend to the rabbit itself unless it too owned the severed leg of one of his mates.

According to hoodoo tradition, the rabbit must be shot with a silver bullet in a cemetery on a rainy Friday during a full moon. Not only that, the leg must be removed while the poor bunny is still alive. Unfortunately you'll need good luck to make sure that it rains on the Friday that coincides with the full moon, so you'll need a rabbit's foot.

Accuracy rating: 3/10

12. Friday the 13th is unlucky

Definitely true if you're hunting rabbits and it's not pissing down with rain.

Accuracy rating: 7/10

13. Warm hands, cold heart

This would be credible if you dropped dead with your fingers clutching a hot water bottle or stuck in a plug socket, but otherwise hands tend to be the same temperature as the rest of the corpse.

Accuracy rating: 2/10

14. If you refuse to kiss under the mistletoe, it's bad luck

One the one hand, what harm could an innocent kiss do? On the other, there's oral herpes and Aunt Victoria's wandering tongue.

Accuracy rating: 5/10

15. If you walk under a ladder, you will have bad luck

Less an old wives tale, and more pretty obvious advice, especially if you're in a slapstick comedy. It's probably also true that if you run blindfold across the M6, eat rat poison, swim The Irish Sea naked or date Alex Reid you'll have just as much bad luck.

Accuracy rating: 9/10

The lesson from most of these seems to be that there are hundreds of very random items waiting to seriously ruin your day, and you need to be paranoid about every single one of them.

Other things thought to bring bad luck include black cats, indoor umbrellas, stepping on cracks in paving stones, singing at the table, sleeping on the table, birds on windowsills, howling dogs, chasing someone with a broom, dropping a dishcloth, a bride not wearing a veil, getting out of bed the wrong side, killing an albatross, rocking an empty rocking chair, wearing opals and giving someone an empty wallet. So if you've done all of those things today, don't expect a major Lotto prize.

And, it seems that old wives tales aren't quite as accurate as we were lead to believe. It only took us a few years to rumble Santa Claus and the Easter Bunny, but illogical parables like all of the above have lingered far too long.

So if you tell the grandchildren about any of these theories, they will rightly think you have lost whatever marbles you had left and need to be committed to a secure unit for your own protection.

So what advice *can* I give?

Let's be honest here – you can choose to give endless advice to everyone in your family, but how much of it will they actually listen to?

Probably not much.

However, there is still an important way you can be of help to your adult children as they struggle with parenthood themselves. It's one of your most important, and satisfying roles.

Namely pointing out all the many ways in which *your* parenting was so much better than *theirs*.

It's surely best that they hear a few home truths from you rather than a child protection agency. That way, they get the chance to act on them before the authorities are tipped off by a concerned neighbour.

The key advantage you have over them is that you are a backseat driver. In other words, you can inflict your advice without ever having to worry about the consequences.

For example, if your daughter told you specifically not to give her children Smarties, and you do so – it's not you who has to deal with the hyperactivity and broken china.

And you didn't do it out of spite – quite the reverse in fact. You were helping her become a better mother by letting her see how erroneous all her rules were. Everyone knows how nutritious Smarties are.

If she chooses to listen and to act upon what she hears, she could become a mother nearly as good as you were.

You'll notice that I'm assuming it's the granny giving advice here to the daughter. Grandads wisely tend to stay clear of such confrontations by going fishing, washing the car or faking an angina attack.

So, rather than giving her a lecture or power point presentation, just drop a few throwaway lines into the conversation. Start in a gentle, reassuring way, and gradually get more direct.

I'm sure you'll agree that none of the following lines could in any way be described as annoying, patronizing, factually incorrect or preachy...

1. Another cold? Why you don't give them caster oil every day, I'll never know.
2. Well, dear, a few dozen smacks on the bottom with a heavy stick never did you any harm.
3. Pish posh! It's not ADD, it's a lack of discipline.
4. For goodness' sake, it's not chronic fatigue, it's pure laziness.
5. Depression? She just needs a kick up the bum.
6. Don't be so paranoid, it's not a melanoma, it's probably just a bit of dried sunburn.
7. Well, I was told to lay you on your front in the cot, and you never died, did you?
8. You're spoiling them with too many presents. All we got was an apple, a gobstopper and a wooden box.
9. Just give him to me! A teaspoon of sherry will get him to sleep.
10. All these silly bike helmets. In my day we were just careful.
11. Little girls need to learn how to cook and look after their brothers.
12. My grandson is *not* gay! And if he is, it's because you wouldn't let me buy him that toy gun. Try feeding him more red meat.
13. My granddaughter is *not* gay! And if she is, it's because you let her breast feed too long. Anyway, a good man will put her straight.
14. I'm not being rude. I just said if you tape his ears to his head each night, he'll endure fewer Dumbo jokes

15. Well, when you were a child, there weren't all these ridiculous inoculations every other week. Huh? I SAID, IN YOUR DAY... Why you can't get a better hearing aid, I don't know.
16. Of course he won't get snatched if he plays on the verge. There are lots of kids in the road who'd get chosen before *him*.
17. No, I did not call him a 'fat little sod'. I merely suggested fourteen fish fingers seemed a lot. And, anyway, he is in no way 'little'.
18. Gluten intolerant? Picky more like.

What can you learn from celebrity grandparents?

As we all know, famous people are better than us in every way. We idolize them, watch their films, read their books, love their TV shows, avidly follow their trials and sneak a look at their sex tapes.

And old celebrities are better still because they've had more marriages, divorces, arrests, heart attacks, custody battles, scandals and face lifts. And, as they are now elderly, they have experienced so much more and are therefore going to make great Grannies and Gramps.

Here are just a few star grandparents who can teach us mere ordinary people how it should be done...

1. Goldie Hawn

The first, and possibly only, rule of grandparenting for Goldie is to always look and behave ten years younger than her daughter so that the attention never strays away from her to the actual grandchild. After all, she's far more interesting and always will be.

What *we* can learn: Act all ditzy, keep your hair dyed blonde and draped over your saggy arms so that no one sees them.

2. Pierce Brosnan

There is absolutely nothing cooler for a young kid than to be able to boast that his Grandpa was 007. He will be the centre of attention, and the most popular boy in school… right up until the moment one of his friends watches Mamma Mia.

What *we* can learn: If you are going to do something embarrassing, do it in the privacy of your shed

3. Saddam Hussein

A proud and loyal family man, Saddam's first priority was always to look after his sons and make sure they had good jobs and nice houses with gold toilet seats. If anyone tried to harm his kin, he would protect them through increasing security, guard dogs and, occasionally, genocide. Consequently his four wives were all looked after, though his gas bill was sometimes a bit high.

What *we* can learn: If you want to live to see your grandchildren grow up, don't murder any Kurds or invade neighbouring countries.

4. Paul Hogan

Realising that his grandchildren might be embarrassed that he was married to a woman his own age, Paul selflessly found a younger model. Whether he said: '*That's* not a wife…*this* is a wife' is unclear.

What *we* can learn: Who better to understand your children than someone nearly the same age as them? And grandkids can be taxing, but not as taxing as the tax office.

5. Harrison Ford

Having Indiana Jones and Han Solo as part of your extended family is something to feel very proud about. When he then marries someone twenty-two years younger, gets an ear pierced and flogs his most famous role to death…he becomes even more awesome.

What *we* can learn: Carpenter granddaddies are still good, even if they're too busy to make you any toys and mumble so quietly that you can't hear them.

6. Kris Jenner

As the matriarch of the Kardashian family, Kris is there to support her family at every opportunity, as long as it's a photo opportunity. Now a granny to Kourtney's little boy, Mason Dash Disick, she can be there to reassure him that one day he'll be able to change his name. And, as The Truman Show demonstrated, there can be no harm in living your life in the full glare of publicity. Her next step must surely be to put bars on the windows of Mason's bedroom and charge admission.

What *we* can learn: If there are a few terrible traumas, hurtful rows and humiliating relationship failures, then it's okay because we'll probably beat Jersey Shore in the ratings.

7. Prince Philip

The Duke of Edinburgh's preferred method of grandparenting was to hold his entire family in contempt and be as embarrassing as humanly possible. If any of his grandkids had ever approached him for some discreet advice, he'd have sent them away with a clip round the ear, a shoe up their arse and warning about where he'd stick the royal scepter if they ever bothered him again.

What *we* can learn: The little urchins should be told whenever they bring shame upon their family, and the nation in general. And be suspicious of slitty-eyed foreigners.

8. Hugh Hefner

There are no grandparents alive today who couldn't learn a thing or two from Mr Playboy. Hugh has shown us all how we can inter-act better with younger generations and understand their needs and concerns (even if their need is for cash and their concern is that he'll have a heart attack while on top). Not only does Hugh understand the needs of those young enough to be his grandchildren, he marries them and pays them to remove their clothes.

What *we* can learn: Sex in you late 80s can make you feel four years younger. And never compromise on the aesthetics of any future wives

9. Gary Glitter

The well-known 70s glamster may have made a few mistakes, but who hasn't? In his defence, he's always up for babysitting, but if you do use him, be aware there is a very real danger that after you've left him alone with your kids, he will creep into their bedrooms and… play them some of his greatest hits. To most, this isn't a chance worth taking.

What *we* can learn: Avoid embarrassing your grandchildren, by checking your hard drive before you take it to be mended.

10. Sarah Palin

These days not enough grandparents shoot moose, deny evolution and run for vice president. And though lots of grandparents do hold tea parties, Sarah went one better and helped found an entire political movement based on them. However, despite a busy schedule of Republican rallies, public appearances, book writing, TV interviews, documentaries and moose hunting, she always makes sure she has time to call the nanny to ask after the kids and check what's for dinner.

What *we* can learn: At close range, with unobstructed views, your best bet is to aim at the moose's neck as the spine and brain are small targets. Though you'll sacrifice some meat, the shoulder shot will also drop the animal quickly. From a broadside position, trace the foreleg up to about one-third of its way into the body. Hit here and you'll break one or both shoulders, and possibly take out part of the heart too.

11. Rod Stewart

When some of your kids are younger than your grandchildren, you know you're doing something right. Rod shows how important it is not to have a vasectomy in case your next wife wants children. With eight offspring from about fourteen wives, Rod gives hope to any old man in leopard skin leggings.

What *we* can learn: Just like cars and toasters, eventually all wives have to be replaced with younger models. And, at some point during our twilight years we all have to stop asking other people if they think we're sexy.

12. Joseph Stalin

Stalin's skills as a grandparent are often overlooked by historians who focus instead on all that bad stuff he did. Yes, he sent whole provinces to their death in his Gulag camps, forced millions more to die in exile and caused famines on a biblical scale, but to his family he was kindly old Grandpa Joe.

What *we* can learn: Only let your grandchildren read books that you have personally vetted. All others should be rewritten or burnt. And never let them near a copy of Animal Farm.

If nothing else, this shows us that all future old wives tales need to be dreamt up by celebrities. They'd probably have a better hit rate than actual old wives, who have better things to think about like how to get their old husbands off the commode without putting their backs out.

It's just possible that there is an obvious famous grandparent whom I have stupidly forgotten here. That's why I've left this large white space (below) before the next chapter starts for you to make your own notes. This will achieve two things:

1) Help you remember how far you got before you fell asleep.
2) Ensure that Amazon refuses to give you a full refund because you have defaced the book.

7

Making your grandchildren actually like you

"Children are a great comfort in your old age - and they help you reach it faster, too."

Lionel Kauffman

"Maybe there is no actual place called Hell. Maybe Hell is just having to listen to our grandparents breathe through their noses when they're eating sandwiches."

Jim Carrey

Did you like your grandparents? I mean really *like* them rather than tolerating their whims. If you did, then it's worth thinking about what it was that they did to make you feel that way.

Was it the endless cuddles, the endless ice cream or the endless stories they told you? Or was it that you could get away with much more at Granny's house than at home?

If you can isolate that 'likeability' factor, then your job is easy – just replicate it*. It worked for you, so it should work again now.

But what if you didn't particularly like them? What if they were urine-scented oldies who you were forced to visit in your Sunday best while they sat in their urine-scented chair and told you the same story they'd told you the week before.

You see in nature, animals two generations apart rarely meet. It's just not natural for a lioness to be stalking a herd of wildebeest only for her grandmother to hobble over farting and scare off the prey.

And an anaconda half way through eating a sheep isn't going to appreciate his grandfather slithering up expecting to be fed too.

No, nature's way is for the ancestors to largely be dead. Even amoebas, once they have divided their membrane into two through asexual reproduction, aren't known for embracing the extended family.

So why are humans different? Why do we cling to our younger generations, care about their well-being and bake them cakes? Surely we should just wander off across a savanna and eek out an existence until we're killed by a predator or die of starvation.

The fact is that a million years of evolution has made us soft. Our ape-like ancestors would turn in their graves ** if they could see us now, erecting granny flats and installing Stannah stairlifts. How does that ensure the preservation of the species?

But, hold on. We're not animals. Or rather, we *are* animals, but we're special, civilized if you will.

The fact we mainly cherish seniors is a good thing. It's what separates us from lions, anacondas and amoebas.***

Our lives are better for the fact that we have more on our mind than mere survival, and care about those who brought up the people who brought us up.

But, getting back to the earlier point, does that mean that we like them?

This is trickier as, unlike friends, you don't choose your grandparents. Therefore it's going to be up to you to make sure you are likeable.

So, what are the ways to bond with them? There are many to consider.

---

* Unless you only liked Gramps because he let you play with his hollow leg, in which case replicating isn't recommended.

** If, that is, they'd cared enough about their dead folk to actually dig graves,. Lazy sods

*** It's possible there are other things separating us from them. For a start, only one of them has legs.

Should you go on holiday with your grandchildren?

The first thing to say about this method of bonding is that it's a decision you probably won't have to make, as few parents really want an old crusty slowing them down while they trek across Patagonia, or have them tutting loudly when they arrive back at the hotel room drunk and wearing the wrong pants. But, more out of duty than anything else, they may decide that taking their widowed old mum is the right thing to do. Just like giving £50 to a homeless shelter, rather than spending it on a couple of rounds of drinks, is the right thing. Right, but not necessarily enjoyable.

Those who do ask Granny to come with them have two possible motives: a) Pity, or b) free babysitting.

One possible exception is if you are fabulously wealthy and spend the summer on your yacht in The Grenadines, in which case your family will graciously condescend to spend their break with you. But even then, they might prefer it if you were on shore leave.

To help you decide whether or not to accept this 'kind' invitation, here is a diary of one lucky gran who got to spend a week with her family in sunny Bali.

June 20th

V excited. Roger just called to say that he and Jane would like me to go on holiday with them!! A whole week with my lovely grandchildren. So generous. It's all a bit last minute, so I've got to pop to Debenhams to get a cossie.

June 22nd

I think I'm all set. My bag is packed and I'll be ready to be picked up tomorrow. Roger got me to transfer the money for the holiday straight into his account. These overseas jaunts are more expensive than you'd think, but it'll be worth every penny.

June 23rd

Well, I got a taxi to the airport in the end as Roger said he didn't want to overload his Range Rover. I saw them at the check in and waved, but they didn't seem to see me. It turned out that I had to take my ticket to a separate desk. Jane said it was because they didn't manage to get five seats together on the plane.

Lovely flight. My seat was at the back between two very large Balinese gentlemen so I didn't get to see much of the family. I tried to find their seats, but the helpful flight attendant told me that I wasn't allowed past the curtain.

June 24th

The hotel is simply lovely. It has palm trees, a pool and lots of restaurants nearby. Can't wait to try a few of them out! Roger, Jane and the kids have a four-room deluxe villa right on the beach! It's bigger than my house I think. As there wasn't enough room for all five of us, Roger kindly booked me into a room in the main block. I must say the bed is very comfortable. I said I didn't mind that the TV doesn't work as I won't have time to watch it anyway. I asked the porter why the room didn't have any windows, and he said it used to be a laundry cupboard. How interesting! He promised he'd get me a fan as there wasn't any air conditioning either, but I'm sure it will be fine.

June 25th

What an exhausting day! Roger knocked on my door first thing and asked if I'd like to spend the day with Allegra and Charlotte. Would I!!! It turned out he and Jane were going on an all-day yacht trip around Labuan Lalang so I'd be in charge.

It was so nice to be able to spend some time with them. Allegra said that she would like to stay in her room watching TV while Charlotte had her heart set on buying something from the gift shop. I said I'd meet them by the pool in an hour or so. I was a bit surprised that they still weren't with me a couple of hours later, so I went to investigate. Allegra (bless her!) was still in front of the television and listening to her ipod. She said she'd only be a while longer so I left her. Charlotte was in the lounge, and didn't she look a picture! She'd bought herself a whole new outfit complete with jewellery and make up. She said she'd charged it all to my room and asked if that was OK. How could I refuse such big doe eyes? She told me she was glad her other grandmother had broken her ankle last week and been unable to come because I was more generous. The cheeky thing then added that she needed a few more Rupiah for a pair of shoes she'd seen, so who was I to say no?

Had a lovely evening in their villa looking after the girls while Roger and Jane went out for dinner at a nearby Indonesian restaurant. I must admit I'd nearly fallen asleep when they got back just before 3am.

June 26th

I was up at 6.30 this morning. Not bad for an oldie! Roger banged on my door until I woke and said that he had managed to book an excursion around all the quaint villages and towns in the lush valleys, stopping off at a beautiful Hindu temple for lunch. Luckily for me he'd found out that there was quite a bit of walking involved so I was to stay at the hotel for another day with the girls. This time they both went off with some friends they'd made the day before so I didn't see them until dinner time. They both said they were bored with the hotel's food so could I take them out somewhere. I put on my best frock and we set off. I suggested a lovely traditional Balinese cafe along the seafront, but in the end, they chose Burger King. My, they both have quite an appetite!

June 27th

The holiday is going so fast! Today, Roger and Jane said they were going to spend the day relaxing in their villa with the girls. I said I might join them as I was a bit tired too, but Jane suggested that I might like to wander into the town on my own. I'm glad I did because it was beautiful. I found a harbourside taverna and tried the local seafood while watching all the fishing boats and yachts. I got chatting to a pleasant lady from Derby who happens to be staying just along the corridor from me. She managed to get a great deal on her room – it was about a quarter of what Roger paid for mine. He'll be horrified when I tell him.

It was funny because on board one of the biggest charter boats, I was sure I saw Jane and Allegra. I called out, but they immediately disappeared below deck! When I got back to the hotel, I knocked on their villa to tell them that they had a doppelganger, but the door was locked so they were all obviously fast asleep.

I got another chance to babysit in the evening. I was going to call for room service, but Roger gave me a lobster and prawns he'd had in the fridge for a couple of days. He suggested I put plenty of chili sauce on before eating them.

June 28th

June 28th

Felt simply awful in the morning, having been up all night being sick. I'd never felt so ill in my entire life. I phoned Roger's villa a few times, but they must have been out. By mid afternoon, I felt even worse so I called the hotel doctor who said I should really go to hospital. I told them to let Roger know because he'd be worried. I was put in a wheel-chair at around 7pm to be taken to the ambulance. I still hadn't been able to contact Roger, but luckily, he and the family were eating at the poolside barbecue. I called out to him and he waved back, pointed at his food and gave me a shrug. I suppose it would have been silly to let it go cold on my account.

June 29th

June 29th

All day in Denpassar General Hospital. The doctors said I drifted in and out of consciousness and was very sick indeed. They got a message back to the hotel because I knew Roger would be climbing the walls with worry.

The nurse told me that he'd said he would try to call in tomorrow when they get back from their trip to Mengwi Royal Temple. Such a kind boy.

June 30th

Roger popped in this morning to see how I was. The others would have come too, but there was a basket weaving demonstration by the beach they didn't want to miss. Roger was very concerned, and anxious for me to come back to the hotel. He said he thought it would do me good to spend the evening on their couch. Apparently he and Jane have tickets to a dance show in Ubud and paying for a babysitter seemed silly if I'm there.

The doctor was adamant that I wasn't well enough, but Roger was very insistent and told him that he would do everything make sure I was OK.

And he was true to his word – when they got back at 1am, it took all his strength to help me out of their spare bed back up to my room.

July 1st

Can't believe it's time to go home already. What a great week we've all had, apart from me spoiling things by getting ill, that is! I packed my suitcase and went down to the lobby. The receptionist said that the family had had to go on ahead to the airport because the limo driver couldn't wait any longer. I was still feeling very weak, but I managed to pull my case a couple of hundred yards along the main road to the bus stop. There's life in the old dog yet!

At the airport, Roger had taken his family into some lounge or other because the flight was delayed, but I was fine perching on a seat at the gate, and the five hours went by surprisingly quickly.

Back at Heathrow, Roger personally pointed out the way to the taxi rank for me so that I didn't get lost. They had a car picking them up, and there was no point in making a detour of nearly a mile to drop me off when the girls were so tired.

July 2ⁿᵈ

I've just written a short note to the family to thank them so much for taking me with them. I saw my doctor this morning and he says I have acute gastro enteritis and possible kidney failure and will probably be in hospital for at least a month. Still, if I do end up needing a new kidney, I know I can always rely on Roger. It's also lucky I kept the receipt for my swimming costume as I was having so much fun, I didn't actually wear it in the end.

Buying presents they might not hate

Another obvious way to bond is to buy them thoughtful gifts. However, as a grandparent, you are expected to buy these at almost every given opportunity. Failure to do so will result in a downgrading of your Triple A rating and probable loss of contact with the entire family.

Whereas *you're* lucky if you get a Terry's Chocolate Orange and a tin of soap for Christmas and birthdays, you need to put aside considerable funds to finance your generosity.

Presents need to be given on the following occasions:

1. Christmas and birthdays (obvious).

Except that you need to give more than you currently do as you are basing that figure on when you were young. An easy way to work out the right amount is this:

a) Set an overall budget for your grandchildren.
b) Realise that this budget must be *per child*.
c) Double it
d) Double it again, you stingy git
e) Add 20% for postage, packing, natty wrapping paper

2. Whenever you have been away from your house overnight.

A weekend with your sister in Croydon still counts as a 'holiday' and therefore you will be expected to bring something back with you

3. When *they* are going on holiday.

Just to wish them well at their all-inclusive 5-star Tahitian resort, a bucket and spade, pack of Top Trumps or My Little Pony will be accepted with gratitude by the kids, and then left at home by their parents.

4. Whenever one of them is sick.

Don't just show up and offer to fill a hot water bottle, bring round a cuddly toy, comic book or bag of sweets. Failing that, try an Avengers hot water bottle.

5. When you are sick.

You can't seriously think they are going to visit you if you don't have a stash of treats to dole out as a small token of your thanks.

6. When they start a new school.

This is a stressful time for them, made less stressful by the purchase of more sweets, a Dora the Explorer pencil case or a 3GB USB stick.

7. When they finish at a school.

Another stressful time, so what are you waiting for?

8. When you take them to the shops.

You can't just nip into the 7Eleven for a carton of milk as that would be mean. Instead take them to the arcade next door where £30 in gold coins played on the right machines could win something very special like a bubble blower or bouncy ball.

9. When you go to church.

No kid wants to sit through all that boring religious drivel without a book to read or puzzle to solve.

10. When they do a job or you.

Mowing lawns, picking up leaves or walking your pug is hard, unrewarding work, so what better way to reward it than with a reward. Cash will usually suffice. Notes, not coins.

11. When they lose their first tooth.

The Tooth Fairy is all very well, but surely an occasion like this needs to be acknowledged by the purchase of an ornate enamel box in which to keep it.

12. Easter.

Easy one this: chocolate eggs. And not those cute, small ones with pictures of baby animals. They want great big ones the size of a microwave oven, except oval.

Other not to be missed opportunities for your kind heartedness to reveal itself include: Chinese New Year, Valentine's Day, Yom Kippur, Ramadan, Diwali, Hogmanay, United Nations Children's Day, Queen's Birthday, Halloween, May Day, Summer Solstice, Winter Solstice, Thanksgiving, Red Nose Day, Hanukkah, anniversary of the Battle of Vimy Ridge, Pancake Day, St Patrick's Day, Martin Luther King Day and Independence Day.

What sort of present should I buy?

Firstly put aside everything you thought you knew about what kids like. There are a few toys that have sadly gone out of fashion. These include:

Hula-hoop	Rocking horse	The Seekers poster
Cowboy costume	Spinning top	Jack in a box
Meccano set	Charlie's Angels	Rolf Harris doll
Stuffed Clangers	jumpsuit	Gollywog
Victorian doll's house	Airfix model	

They have been replaced by a new generation of play things that reflect society today. Boys are perhaps easier than girls. When in a toy shop agonizing over what to buy for a boy, just follow this flowchart:

Is the toy linked to warfare and killing people
Yes – continue
No – Could it nevertheless join a makeshift toy army?
      Yes – continue
      No – put back on shelf

Will his parents approve of it?
Yes – put back on shelf
No – continue

Does it look like it would survive being dropped from a bedroom window?
Yes – onto concrete?
      Yes – continue
      No – put back on shelf
No – put back on shelf

Is any part of it pink?
Yes – could the pink area be concealed?
      Probably – continue
      Unlikely – put back on shelf
No - continue

Could the toy be used to inflict pain?
Yes – continue
No – Even if thrown at close range?
      Yes – continue
      No – put back on shelf

Has the toy been advertised on every TV channel for the last six months making it a 'must have' item and therefore ludicrously over priced?
Yes – continue
No – put back on shelf

Is the toy endorsed by a action star/sporting hero, or linked to a major blockbuster movie and therefore ludicrously overpriced?
Yes – Is the sporting star Shane Warne?
        Yes – put back on shelf
        No – continue
No – put back on shelf

Is the toy at all educational?
Yes – put back on shelf
No – buy it

For girls, follow this chart:

Is the toy a lovely pastel colour?
Yes – continue
No – put back on shelf

Does it involve make-up, ponies, dolls, hair beading or plastic jewellery?
Yes – continue
No – put back on shelf

If it is clothing, in your day would it have been considered overtly risqué and wholly inappropriate for a young lady?
Yes – continue
No – put back on shelf

Is it endorsed by either Katy Perry, Kristen Stewart, Justin Bieber or The Powerpuff Girls?
Yes – continue
No – put back on shelf

Is it endorsed by Cilla Black, Danielle Lloyd or Vicki Michelle?
Yes – put back on shelf
No – buy it.

How do you know if you got it right?

Watching a child excitingly unwrapping a present on Christmas morning and seeing their face light up in sheer delight… is probably not that likely. Instead, be content if they acknowledge its existence and don't dissolve in tears of disappointment.

To judge how successful your purchase was, match their response to this list below:

Reaction: Oh, wow! Thank you so, so much Gran and Grandad, that is the most awesome present ever! I absolutely love it. You are simply the best.
What they're really thinking: Oh God, they really bought me that? I must seriously overcompensate and pretend that I like it to mask the crushing feeling inside

Reaction: That's…lovely. Thank you, er, so much for it. It's just so… lovely
What they're really thinking: This time I really can't mask the horror I'm feeling.

Reaction: Er, OK. It's definitely for me? Definitely? Well, that is such a surprise. I really had no idea I was going to get that

What they are really thinking: How can these old people have known me all these years and still bought me *that*. Are they more senile than I suspected?

Reaction: You know what, that is a really kind thought, it's just that I have one just like it. Don't suppose you still have the receipt, do you?
What they are really thinking: Maybe I can salvage something from this

Reaction: Cheers, Gran, Gramps. Nice one
What they are really thinking: Finally, you've got it right! This grandchild is genuinely chuffed, and doesn't feel the need to exaggerate his feelings for effect. The same is true if all you get is a grunt or mumble.

In conclusion, it is very difficult to *make* someone like you if you're not actually very likeable. This leaves you two options: Become more likeable or fake likeability by masking all the aspects of your character that right-thinking people deem 'not likeable'.

To make it easier, think about people you know whom everyone despises: Social lepers, misfits, pariahs, Millwall fans and compensation lawyers. What is it about them that causes such contempt?

If you can isolate it, then you can look at yourself and realise how much more your grandchildren would like you if you made one or two minor adjustments.

Things like:

a) Occasionally turn off your electric fence
b) Clip the hedge so it looks less like a swastika
c) Mop up the blood on the drive when you spear a baby squirrel
d) Be more discrete about leaving the waste from your vivisection experiments out with your dustbins.
e) Re-record your answerphone message so it contains fewer references to Sodom and Gomorrah

f) Consider changing the cat's name from Adolf
g) When a ball is accidentally kicked into your garden, occasionally return it without knife wounds.

You'll soon get the idea. And anyway, if you bought this book, it suggests to me that you are very likeable because you really want to be a truly outstanding grandparent. An unlikeable person wouldn't have wasted his or her money*

However, if someone bought this for *you*...

* Not that purchasing this book could ever be construed as a waste of money. For a start, for every copy sold, I'm putting a pound towards eradicating small pox in the Isle of Wight.

8

How to Survive Babysitting

"On the seventh day, God rested. His grandchildren must have been out of town."

"My grandkids believe I'm the oldest thing in the world. And after two or three hours with them, I believe it, too."

Gene Perret

The advantage/disadvantage of living close to your adult children is that you get to spend quality time with the grandkids while babysitting. Quality, *and* quantity.

Except that there really isn't much quality as such, unless you count the hours they are asleep.

For a start, the children will be overtired, pissed off their parents are abandoning them and angry that they have to go to bed. Happily, all this pent up aggression will be unleashed on you. You may have generously given up your free time so that your daughter can have an evening of pampering at the local spa or your son can drink twenty pints of Stella down the Royal British Legion, but don't expect any thanks from your charges.

So, if you've just been asked to mind the precious little mites for the first time, you need to be forewarned and (literally) forearmed.

And don't expect much actual 'sitting'. More than likely you will be expected to do a whole lot more than plonk yourself down in front of The One Show with a cup of coffee.

To illustrate how this will almost certainly play out, take this real-life example of a kindly, but arguably naïve, Nanna enjoying an evening's babysitting*

* Names have been changed because it's only loosely based on real events. Or possibly it's fictitious.

7pm

You arrive to find both parents waiting by the front door, checking their watches with the clear implication that you're late, which means they are late too, so you have been selfish.

7.01pm

You are given a barrage of information and expected to remember every single detail on pain of death. It'll sound something like this:

'Oh hi, Mum, look we've got to rush. James is in his pyjamas, but hasn't had tea so give him something from the fridge, or a tin of something, or… something. Timmy is due back from cubs any moment, get him showered and into bed. If he's hungry, whip him up something quick and tell him to finish his homework on the worksheet, numbers 23-41, and then the second half of Section 4f and stick it into his book. The Sellotape is in the drawer, or his cupboard or, er…. He must be asleep by 8.15pm. Did I say James's new bedtime is 7.15pm, so you'll need to hurry? Emily is refusing to come out of the bathroom, she needs her uniform ironing – you don't mind, do you? – and reading a story. It must be the one she's doing at school. It's called…er, something to do with trees, or boats, I think. The dog hasn't been fed and Muffie the rabbit needs its flea spray and some new hay. The shopping's being delivered between 7.30pm and 8pm, so make sure the frozen stuff gets put away – if you can pay I'll settle up when I've got some cash - and Tom from next door wants to borrow our strimmer, so you can dig it out of the shed for him if you like, I think it's behind all the bikes. Help yourself to biccies. We'll try not to be late. Oh, and James wet the bed last night, so it may need changing. Leave the pile of dog sick in the utility, unless you get a spare moment, that is. Bye!'

7.03pm
   A quick inspection of the biscuit barrel reveals it is empty.

7.04pm
   James complains he feels sick and wants a bucket by his bed. Emily says she's only coming out of the bathroom if she can have her Malibu Barbie back. She has no idea where it is.

7.05pm
   Timmy arrives back from cubs, walks through the dog sick and leaves a trail all the way up the stairs. James vomiting down toilet, while an initial search for Malibu Barbie proves fruitless.

7.06pm
   Timmy demands fish fingers and chips, James thinks he's OK now so you dress him in a new pair of pyjamas. Dog spotted eating some of James' sick so is banished into the garden.

7.10pm
   Negotiations with Emily stall as she admits the doll could be any-where, but blames you for not looking hard enough. Smoke alarm goes off as the fish fingers turn black in the pan. Three new ones are put on.

7.12pm
   James calls down from his room to say he's been sick all over his bed. You lie to Emily that Malibu Barbie has been found. She demands you hold it up so she can see through the keyhole. You raise

your voice and order her out or you'll call her father and he'll deal with her. She laughs.

7.17pm

James' bedclothes have been changed and a new pair of pyjamas found. He asks for a story and bursts into tears and says he'll be sick again when you refuse. Through gritted teeth, you rush through the shortest Dr Seuss you can find.

7.20pm

Second round of fish fingers burnt to a crisp, none left in freezer. Timmy explodes in anger and says he wishes his other grandmother was here.

7.22pm

Search of freezer uncovers a pizza and a few chips. This is agreeable to Timmy. James calling down for water. You tell Emily that if she doesn't come out you will throw away her dolls house. To add credence to this, you make her watch you through the keyhole taking it downstairs.

7.23pm

Emily emerges from bathroom. You sit Timmy down to do homework, which he refuses point blank. Threat to abort the pizza changes his mind.

7.27pm

Timmy says he forgot to put Muffie in her cage. In a panic, you rush out into the yard to see the dog burrowing under the rhododendron. No sign of rabbit. You grab the dog's tail, but it wriggles free so you dive under the branches just in time to stop it getting the rabbit. You hear the doorbell.

7.28pm

You run back inside to open the door for the shopping delivery and see Emily disappearing upstairs clutching the doll's house. You breathlessly say to the driver: 'Gotta… go garden..dog… and..rabbit.. Kitchen.. that… way. Sorry…'

As he doesn't speak much English, he looks perplexed and gives you a form to sign. You grab it, frantically try to sign your name, but the pen doesn't work. You run it up and down all over the form, but nothing.

You make back for the garden, and notice Timmy asleep at the table. You shake him awake, point to Section 4g and warn him that there will be no pizza unless it's done. You then grab his pencil, sign the shopping form, run out the door and dive back under the bush.

7.29pm

The dog is inches away from Muffie who has managed to squeeze up against the corner of the fence. You smack the dog, and break off a branch to prod him. He starts growling, but you manage to grab Muffie and pull him into your stomach. At that moment, you hear a voice asking you if it's OK to substitute Sainsbury's own peach slices for Del Monte.

7.30pm

The dog goes for the delivery man, who fends him off by throwing the tin of peaches at him. Still grasping the rabbit, you stagger towards the back door. Emily shouts from bathroom window that she has taken the doll's house hostage and is hungry. James appears in doorway and says he has wet his bed again.

7.32pm

Placing the rabbit in the washing machine to keep her safe, you shoe the dog outside, find your purse to pay for the shopping and once again yell out to Timmy to wake up. James asks why there's smoke coming out of the oven.

7.35pm

As delivery van pulls away, another man appears at the front door asking if you've managed to find the strimmer. You point towards the garage, open the oven door and the kitchen is filled with a black plume of smoke. The chips are thrown into the bin and you notice James is standing by the back door naked. You tell him to find some more pyjamas while you get the pizza out of the oven. It's not burnt!

7.39pm

Attempts to revive Timmy prove futile. You drag him upstairs, put him on his bed and, as you struggle to put his pyjamas on, you feel a muscle in your back go. After collapsing to the floor in agony, Emily shouts that she's not coming out until she has some food. James says there are no more pyjamas and the neighbour bellows up the stairs that he can't find the strimmer.

7.42pm

Screaming thinly veiled threats of violence fails to get Emily out of the bathroom. She says she wants food and her Barbie or she'll tell her mum that you nearly killed Muffie.

7.45pm

Now in even greater agony, you make it downstairs and find James still naked and shivering. He is ordered to bed and bursts into tears. The neighbour appears and asks if you have a torch.

7.48pm

You manage to slide the pizza under the bathroom door as Emily has sworn on her brownie's honour that she will come out if you do. When she gets it, she rudely demands ketchup with it.

7.51pm

You get a t-shirt and pants for James to wear in bed, and find more sheets for his bed. He is near hysterical with tiredness, cold and hunger. You ask Emily if James can have some of the pizza, but she refuses unless she gets ketchup. Neighbour asks if you managed to find the torch.

7.56pm

Ketchup squirted onto piece of kitchen roll and pushed under the door. No pizza appears in return. You tell her she has two minutes to push some out or you will break down the door.

7.59pm

Search of garage commences. After five minutes of clambering over lawnmower, garden chairs, fishing rods and work benches, you find it and pass it to the neighbour. He thanks you and exits, leaving you stuck.

8.07pm

You try to ignore the searing pain and scramble your way out of the garage and find James downstairs eating Frosties. Still no pizza from bathroom. Emily refuses to answer. You think you hear the sound of snoring from the other side of the door. Doorbell goes and neighbour standing there asking if you have any petrol for the strimmer as it's empty.

8.21pm

James finally in bed. Dog allowed back inside. It has a chewed up and headless Malibu Barbie between its teeth.

8.27pm

Exhausted, and still in hideous pain, you slump onto a sofa, only to remember all the wet bedclothes. In a daze, you shove them into the washing machine, straining your back still further, and put them on to an express cycle.

8.56pm

It has taken you half an hour to crawl to the sitting room and haul yourself up onto the sofa. The pain is worse than anything you've ever experienced. Dog sits in front of you, looking hungry. You tell it to get lost, but it refuses to budge.

9.12pm

Getting the dog food takes you another 15 minutes. Once it is put in the bowl in front of the dog, he sniffs it, walks off and climbs on to the sofa.

9.20pm

Finally you get back to a comfy chair. Timmy walks in and says he's scared there is a monster in his wardrobe. You stagger upstairs, check the wardrobe and reassure him. He says you must stay with him in case it comes back just as James calls out that he's been sick again. You notice the bathroom door is open, and the tiled floor is covered with tomato sauce, which looks at first glance to be blood. Timmy notices it and screams in terror and refuses to believe it's only a condiment.

Dog charges upstairs, still holding doll. Emily appears and faints. You hear the front door open and your daughter call out: 'Hi Mum, everything OK?'

Babysitting: the rules

This all-too-typical scenario shows that, when it comes to babysitting, you cannot be too careful. It is not an activity to be taken on lightly. You wouldn't climb Mount Everest without crampons and warm gloves, would you?

Well, don't agree to mind your children's children until you realize the following:

1. Your son/daughter will assume that you are on call 24 hours a day, 364 days a year. The other day is Christmas Day when they will announce they are coming round to yours for lunch.
2. Not only that, you will be required to be available at a moment's notice.
3. Not only *that*, it will be further taken for granted that you will never tire of coming round, even at a rate of six times a week.
4. And, not only all those other things, babysitting is *them* doing *you* a favour. How generous of your son to give you the chance to see your angelic grandchildren for the fifth consecutive night when he could have been mean and actually paid someone to do it.
5. Most importantly, if you cannot babysit because you are looking after your *other* grandchildren, you are playing favourites again, just like you did when your kids were growing up, and this only proves what a bad mother you were so you should feel very lucky that you are allowed anywhere near your grandchildren

Is it ever OK to refuse to babysit?

You really have to ask? Of course it is, you idiot. In fact refusal should be actively encouraged or else you'll end up like one of the maids in Downton Abbey facing a lifetime of servitude, fatigue and orders barked by an overweight butler.

However, if you are going to dare to say no, it is best to give a valid reason so it's not seen as an unforgivable act of defiance.

Possible excuses to proffer include:

1. My gammy knee is still weeping pus, and I'm worried about your carpet.
2. Darn it! Me and Betty start our pathology class that night.

3. Tuesday? Sorry, that's when I check your dad's back for melanomas

4. My horoscope says I might be a danger to Taureans like baby Harry on the 13th

5. I'll still be holding a vigil at the church for Julian Assange

6. I'd be there like a shot if it didn't violate the terms of my Witness Protection Order.

7. If you're happy to risk me passing on viral hepatitis B, then I'll be there at 7pm.

8. Sorry, but the anniversary of the date Kajagoogoo split up is still too painful.

9. Is it Ok if I bring along that death row prisoner I was corresponding with? He got off on a technicality. Oh, Ok, he escaped.

10. I think your house is more than a kilometer away from mine so my court ordered electronic angle tag may go off.

None of these should arouse any suspicion, but be careful not to overuse them or else they'll have you sussed.

If, of course, you decide that you would after all like to babysit on this occasion, then that's lovely. Lovely and brave. Lovely, brave and inherently risky.

Before you turn up, just get your solicitor to courier over this contract for them to sign so there can be no misunderstandings, court cases or loss of life.

BABYSITTING TERMS AND CONDITIONS

THIS DOCUMENT SETS OUT THE RULES FOR ALL FUTURE CHILD-MINDING DUTIES BETWEEN .... (YOUR NAME, HEREAFTER REFERRED TO AS 'GRANNY OR GRAMPS') AND .... (NAMES OF GRANDCHILDREN, HEREAFTER REFERRED TO AS 'THOSE KIDS')

We the undersigned hereby agree that when Granny or Gramps are asked to babysit, the following conditions will be agreed to. Failure to conform to one or more of these as set out below will result in legal action/punitive damages/formal apology/unholy row (delete as appropriate).

1. More than fifteen minutes notice will be given when requesting babysitting services. Using the words 'I know it's really late notice, and I'm really sorry' does not mitigate this point.
2. Adequate refreshments will be provided. Specifically mint tea, fair trade coffee and at least four of those nice oatmeal biscuits with the gooey caramel bits inside. A doily-covered plate will also be made available.
3. Granny and Gramps will not be expected to carry out any of the following additional duties:
    i) Re-dress the wound on the cat's right leg
    ii) Explain the reasoning behind Gramps' unusual neck tattoo
    iii) Respond to the myna bird's bad language
    iv) Loan Gramps' false arm for the purpose of playing Twister.
    v) Be asked to give any dead goldfish a 'decent burial'
    vi) Sit through the video of Mummy giving birth to little Ruby.

4. Indemnity against all breakages, spillages and injuries caused by those kids.
5. Further, if injury occurs to Granny or Gramps, they will be compensated according to the following scale:
6.
    i) Broken fingernail (Granny only): £25
    ii) Cut requiring stitches: £50
    iii) Significant bruise or puncture wound caused by projectile: £60
    iv) Broken rib (£75 per rib to maximum £450)
    v) Major head injury: £300 (Granny), £150 (Gramps)

vi)   Loss of limb: £1000

vii) Death from heart failure £1050

7. No creased clothes will be casually left on the ironing board in the sitting room.

8. When you say, you 'might be a bit late', this doesn't mean you'll fall in the door steaming drunk at 5am and vomit over Gramps' slippers.

9. The location of the TV remote will be ascertained *before* you leave house so that other options beyond the Cartoon Network are available.

10. No padlock will mysteriously appear on the drinks cabinet prior to the arrival of the sitters. Nor will the 18-year-old Scotch be hidden in the cupboard under the stairs again.

11. The Alsatian will be placed outside if the hum from Gramps' hearing aid provokes it to howl or launch another attack.

Signed   date

....

(The babysitters)   (the babysitees)

Witnessed by...............

What if they stay with *me*?

Yes, babysitting has an even darker side: the home invasion. Instead of you sitting on their couch for a few hours before exiting safely, they might be the ones perching on *your* couch. And not only perching on it – sticking gum underneath it, resting their muddy shoes on the throw cushions and jumping up and down until a spring snaps.

We touched briefly on preparing your house for a baby in Chapter 2, but when the baby becomes a child, and then the child becomes a brat, the experience can be a whole lot more traumatic.

The danger zones are:

1. Anything breakable
2. Anything not breakable that can be used to break something breakable
3. Pets
4. Food
5. Furniture that isn't nailed down and made from reinforced steel.

Before they arrive, quickly go through this 10-point checklist:

1. Is the budgie cage locked?
2. Are the posh biscuits well enough hidden?
3. Have the neighbours been warned?
4. Have you dug out the framed photos of the kids about to visit and placed them in prominent positions?
5. Are your earplugs and Valium within easy reach?
6. Are there enough DVDs to last six hours?
7. Have you concealed the 'special' DVD the two of you made that time.
8. Have you put Gramps' Viagra tablets on a high enough shelf?
9. Will you remember where you put them in case he gets back from the pub in one of his frisky moods?
10. Does the Naughty Step still have its ankle chains attached?

How to make them scared of your fridge

One thing children will always demand is food. And neither your freshly chopped carrot sticks nor a bunch of grapes will be considered edible.

If a plate of something either deep fried or containing 99% sugar isn't apparent, then they will go in search of it. And their Holy Grail is the fridge.

Assuming that you can't fit a padlock, you need to make sure that they don't get close enough to inflict a scorched earth policy on what's inside.

The best way to achieve this is to make them actually scared of the fridge. Or at least to cast a shadow of doubt over what might lurk inside.

Simply cut out one or more of these notices and Blu-Tack them on the front.

Warning!
Do not defrost human head

Please remove dwarf <u>before</u> climbing inside

Danger!
Gateway to Narnia
(sulky queen inside)

STOP!
Pathology samples can look like regular food

Fridge will **EXPLODE** on opening

Property of *Basingstoke Sperm Bank*
<u>Do not remove!</u>

Turn back, Fatso
- no one likes an obese kid

How should you punish them?

When you tell off your own kids, anything goes. You're in charge, and you have no one to answer to, except perhaps the police if the child get regression therapy in later life and remembers the cat o' nine tails.

But when it comes to inflicting mental or physical suffering on someone else's child, the rules change. Suddenly the person who you once smacked on the bum has a say on how you do the smacking.

And of course, smacking is a big no no these days, as apparently it will lead to the child becoming a psychopath, sociopath and very possibly an osteopath.

So, to help you decide on what punishment to hand out next time you are babysitting, feel the anger welling up and notice a claw hammer within your reach, make sure you have this handy quiz about your person...

1. Is this the first time the child has committed the offence?
    Yes -6 points
    First time today -1
    No + 6 points
    Who gives a shit? + 10 points

2. Did any family pets perish?
    Only next door's hamster + 1 point
    No, but the micro pig has a flesh wound + 5 points
    I can't find the corgi, and there's a funny smell coming from the microwave + 10 points

3. Was anything valuable damaged?
    Slight blood stain on the antique Moroccan rug + 8 points
    Slight blood stain on the pieces of the 18th century Staffordshire bone china vase scattered on the rug + 12 points
    Slight blood stain above the right ear of the unidentified corpse lying amid the bone china on the rug + 14 points

4. Does the child appear remorseful?
    Yes, he hasn't stopped crying since I belted him up the backside
    – 4 points
    A bit, though he's already uploaded the incident onto Youtube.
    + 3 points
    No, he's made his four-year-old sister sign an affidavit implicating
    you + 6 points

5. Did the child admit their actions were wrong?
    Only after a five-hour interrogation – 1 point
    Only after you agreed a plea bargain - + 1 point
    Only after you'd extracted a fingernail. + 2 points

6. Do the child's parents approve of corporal punishment
    Yes, er, well... they *might* + 2 points
    No, they believe in reasoning with the child – 6 points
    Did you say capital punishment? + 7 points

7. How would *you* have dealt with it when *you* had young kids?
    Threatened them with a lump of hardboard 0 points
    Threatened them with boarding school + 1 point
    Threatened them with waterboarding + 12 points

8. Rate your level of anger
    Bit peeved - 10 points
    Homicidal + 10 points
    Genocidal + 50 points

How you rated
Less than zero : Count to ten, have a coffee and make them sit on
the Naughty Step for ten minutes. If that doesn't work, clip them round
the ear.

Zero to 20: Kids need a firm hand, and you know exactly where to put that hand. Just be aware that their parents might not let you baby-sit again if you smack them. So make sure you don't leave bruising. Better still, punish them by making them file down that callus on your heel.

Over 20: This little brat only understands one language, and you need some come down on it like a ton of bricks. So use those bricks to convert your basement into a makeshift dungeon and suspend the child upside down in chains. Its parents will probably thank you*

* inwardly thank you, outwardly have you locked up for child abuse

If the unavoidable truth is that you really can't punish them in any way for fear of judicial repercussions, then it does take half the fun out of from babysitting. And half of not very much is even less.

On the other hand, there's nothing to stop you making veiled threats, as long as the recipients of said threats don't realise they are entirely hollow.

Effective ones include telling them you will:

- Send them to bed early
- Confiscate a treasured cuddly toy
- Make them to sit at the bottom of the stairs
- Make them to sit half way up their stairs if they can still see the TV from the bottom.
- Refuse them a slice of your homemade date and cashew sponge
- Make them actually eat a slice of your homemade date and cashew sponge
- Set fire to a treasured cuddly toy
- Tell Mummy about hitting their brother
- Tell Mummy about impaling their brother
- Disembowel a treasured cuddly toy

- Tell Mummy where they've buried their brother
- Make their treasured cuddly toy eat a slice of your date and cashew sponge

Soon you'll have them eating out of the palm of your hand*

* As long as it doesn't contain a slice of your date and cashew sponge

9

Grandchildren from broken homes

Happiness is having a large, loving, caring, close-knit family in another city.
George Burns

"If a man is found sleeping with another man's wife, both the man who slept with her and the woman must die."
Deuteronomy 22:22

Ok, let's first get the obvious joke out of the way – when grandchildren are involved, most of the contents of a home will be broken anyway. Boom boom. And, I suppose, if you need to split said contents in half, it helps if several items have already been snapped into two.

It used to be that humans would mate for life (like swans and Catholics) and endure the thick and thin that marriage brings. For every bad year, you probably got a few weeks of good, and for every row there was at least the prospect of make up sex.

These days, it's not so much 'til death us do part', as 'til he leaves his ear wax in the sink one more time us do part'.

Which is a bit sad…unless you're a divorce lawyer or a reality TV producer.

In fact maybe it's the media that causes all this. When women see Katie Price or Kim Kardashian picking up and discarding husbands every other week, perhaps it plants a seed. A seed that suggests they'd like someone else's seed planted in them from now on.

And the Internet has meant that cheating for a bloke can be done from the comfort of your laptop rather than from the comfort of the back seat of your car in a dark, wooded area.

So being unfaithful is easier than ever, and most wives are still wedded* to the naïve notion that if a bloke has an affair then divorce is the only option.

As mums and dads split up, remarry other mums and dads, have more kids in their second, third and fourth marriages, adopt their new partner's kids, have lesbian affairs, reverse their vasectomies and pay for surrogate kids, so family trees start looking like a plate of spaghetti**.

Could it be that the Mormons have got it right? Instead of having only one wife, have five – one for every weekday. Then no one is forced to spend every day with the same spouse so the rows become less. Best of all, you still get a weekend***.

But however it happens, when parents split, it's very traumatic for the children. Their little lives are suddenly shattered. And, with two parents screaming obscenities and death threats at each other, it will be you who will have to step in to support them (and subtly convince them that it's your son or daughter they need to side with, not the scary son or daughter-in-law).

* On reflection, use of the word 'wedded' was unfortunate there.
** Without the sauce
*** And a weak end if you've serviced all five wives.

Children will have so much running their through tiny heads. Things like:

1. Should I live with Mummy or Daddy? What if I hate them both?
2. But I thought they were getting on much better as Mummy had stopped screaming and bouncing on the bedsprings in the bedroom.
3. Will I be allowed to split my brother down the middle?

4. Please say we don't have to move house – all my pets are buried in the garden. And some might still be alive.
5. Is it because Daddy hasn't washed enough? I just heard Mum say she was going to take him to the cleaners
6. Is it all my fault? If so, can I pin it on little Jimmy instead?
7. Who will get the rabbit? Can I get one of his legs as a lucky charm?
8. How the hell are we going to pass the time with Dad every other Saturday?
9. Mum's always crying these days. Is it because she's worried she won't be able to afford my gymkhana lessons? Or because Dad's shagging the barmaid at the Horse and Plough?
10. Dad's always drinking these days. At least that explains the heifer we caught him banging in his car in a dark, wooded area last week.

How to reassure them (and not miss too much TV)

You will be there to convince them that they needn't worry and that everything is going to be OK.

In the end. Almost certainly.

When they come to you while you're trying to watch Home and Away, palm them off with a few of these helpful phrases:

Hey, dry those tears, little one. You'll need to save some for when things get *really* bad.

Of course Daddy still loves all of you. It's just that his new bikini model can do things you guys can't

You're going to have to be strong for Mummy. Especially when you're lugging all that furniture out of your bedroom.

Your new house will be just as lovely, and I'll visit as soon as Rentokil have been round.

Yes, we were all a bit surprised when Mummy moved in with Bertha, but now you have two mums, and one of them loves you very much.

I know you're terribly upset and just want to sit on your own and eat muffins. But Daddy's new wife won't want a fat child, now, will she?

Let's go to the park and play catch to take our minds off it. And by 'park' I mean the only place you'll see your father from now on.

I just think they grew apart. That happens to mummies and daddies sometimes. Especially when one is serving three life sentences for heroin smuggling and attempted murder.

Of course there's a chance that they might get back together one day...if Mummy hits her head and gets complete amnesia.

It's called a custody battle, dear, to decide who looks after you. You'll end up living with whoever loses.

No, no, no, Mummy was only joking when she said she wanted to plunge a bread knife into Daddy's heart and twist it until he was dead! And anyway, a carving knife would work better...

If all else fails, sit them in front of Kramer vs Kramer and they'll know what to expect. Once a few weeks have passed, Daddy has moved out and the Sky sports channels have mysteriously stopped working, it will get easier.

Easier for them, but not for you. Suddenly your grandchildren will be under the care of someone who has probably resented and distrusted you from the start (no, not *your* child, the one he married).

And the days of popping over unannounced are over. Whereas *her* parents will have a door key, and spend birthdays, Christmas and holidays with them, you are now in the enemy camp.

On the up side, your son will have more free time to mow your lawn, but that is scant compensation.*

So, you need a strategy. Something that will convince her to let you see your extended family more than every other leap year. She will become immediately suspicious if you suddenly start bringing round freshly baked pies and knitted bootees**, and even *she's* not going to be fooled into thinking that you suddenly love babysitting***.

Instead, help her to see the advantages to her in your continued existence in her life. And, when you have her attention, pull a few heartstrings to seal the deal.

* Unless he digs the beds too
** Especially if she doesn't actually have a baby
*** Possibly because you were dumb enough to use one of the excuses in the last chapter

Start by trying out a few of these...

Fool your daughter-in-law into letting you have access

1. I realise the last thing you want now is for us to be popping round getting under your feet as we tend the garden, do the washing and clean the house
2. I suppose that useless son of mine hasn't even told you that my beloved Great Aunt Doris died. She had no children, so it's anyone's guess who'll be left her mansion and stud farm.

3. If my son isn't paying you enough, leave it with me. He's drinking so heavily these days, I can get him to agree to anything.

4. Sorry I'm late, my dear, I got talking to my new neighbour. He's recently divorced too and says he's desperate to get a steady girlfriend but as a millionaire plastic surgeon and former underwear model, he finds it difficult to met the right girl, especially with his sex addiction.

5. I know it's the third time this week I've been over. I just want to pack as much in as I can as the doctor says I'll be dead in three months.

6. I haven't forgotten that you've been sober for a year now, but one bottle of vodka can't hurt. I'll get the glasses and then we can have a natter about me getting a key cut.

7. You won't be letting me take them to church anymore? OK, but don't say I didn't warn you that they'll burn in the fires of hell with Lucifer for all eternity. Also, the Sunday school has a new cookie-making machine!

8. Look, I'll be honest – there are a lot of drug gangs on this estate, and I know some people who can make sure you're looked after. Just tell me how many grams you want, and I'll get you a good price.

9. I don't give a damn what everyone else thinks, I think you're a good mum.

The final thing to say about the human tragedy of divorce is that it means you'll only see the grandkids every *other* Christmas. So, in the years they are with the other grandparents, make sure you buy them the biggest, most expensive presents you can afford to cement your position as 'the favourite'.

Just for fun, it's also worth considering getting them something to unwrap that is clearly going to piss off their parent. I'm not saying you *should* do this because it's actually very petty and childish. I just that you *might*. It's a free country.

Anyway, here are a few ideas of things that you would never be evil enough to purchase.

Drum kit
Pet snake
Realistic toy gun
Huge bag of sweets
Whoopee cushion
Violent console game
Stink bomb
The Tweenies' Greatest Hits
Hunger Games bow and arrow
Membership of a cage fighting club
Cans of spray paint
Fifty Shades of Grey duvet cover
Play swords
Voucher for tattoo parlour

Made a note? Good, now rip out and eat this page so no one knows where you got such wicked thoughts. And I mean 'wicked' in the bad sense of the word in case that wasn't clear.

10

Dealing with Conflict So It Looks Like It's Not Your Fault

"The reason grandparents and grandchildren get along so well is that they have a common enemy."

Sam Levinson

"I phoned my grandparents and my grandfather said 'We saw your movie.' 'Which one?' I said. He shouted 'Betty, what was the name of that movie I didn't like?'."

Brad Pitt

There are few certainties in life – night follows day, the speed of light is constant, Paul McCartney looks like a lesbian and mothers won't get on with the woman who took away their precious son and married him.

Like two bull elephants in the same enclosure, they will pace around each other suspiciously before one lunges in trunk first.*

The mother thinks her son isn't being fed properly (or is being over-fed), that the grandchildren run wild (or that she's too strict with them) and the house is too messy (or she's too obsessive about housework).

Meanwhile the daughter-in-law is paranoid that her husband's mother thinks she's not feeding him properly, the grandchildren are running wild and that the house is a mess.

This goes back to what we discussed in earlier chapters about old people being convinced the Olden Days were better and that their methods the best, and young parents trying to explain how child rearing has moved on since the Middle Ages.

Skirmishes are inevitable, and these will mostly occur in the kitchen. It's been said that two women can't share a kitchen, and science will almost certainly prove that to be true one day. However, if you're a bloke, avoid saying that one woman in the kitchen is the perfect scenario as that's old fashioned apparently.

So, just as two faiths may struggle to coexist alongside each other, the same is true for two females. The only difference is that the fall out from two women, er, falling out is far greater than any religious-based atrocity.

But, we're assuming here that the relationship has broken down to such a point that open warfare has been declared. In practice, this is rare. A more likely outcome is that the two of them will get on just fine. In the same way two ferrets get on until they're put down the same trousers.

The daughter-in-law from Hell

From your perspective, how do you get on with this objectionable witch without upsetting your son? Because we all know who's side he'll take. To be fair to him, he does have to live with her, so some self-preservation is understandable. Deep down he surely agrees with you, but he can't express it for fear of reprisals.

You need to be able to handle this woman without it looking like you are, in any way, handling her.

So, you pretend everything is coming up roses, but carefully get in enough digs** to counter the ones she'll be throwing back at you.

---

* When trying to quell a argument between any two women, best not use bull elephants as your example. Seahorses will do just as well (though remember they don't have trunks)

** Just don't dig up the roses or you'll have a very confused metaphor.

Start with a few of these:

1. That's a lovely dress, Jackie, it's so nice to give to charity
2. Oh good gracious, you've actually done your hair. What an unusual colour – what did it say it was on the bottle?
3. I suppose we *could* try some of your soufflé, though Max has cross country tomorrow and I think it'll still be lodged in his stomach.
4. Tom, my love – you look stunning as usual. Sarah – you look...as usual.
5. Oh it's your *perfume*! My mistake, I thought someone was marinating goat meat
6. You want my son to have a vasectomy? Is that fair on his next wife?
7. No, honestly, that dress doesn't make you look fat. You looked just as big before you put it on.

If these don't work, you will have to call an uneasy truce. You agree to abide by each other's rules, when visiting. Draw up a chart just in case.

You promise...

1. Not to draw unnecessary attention to any disastrously burnt meals.
2. That you will warn Gramps not to cough phlegm all over the trifle
3. To not mention any of you son's ex girlfriends in a favourable light
4. In fact, not to mention them at all, in any light.
5. Well, unless the light is overwhelmingly unfavourable. Then it might be OK.

6. To suggest in any way that you know your son better than she does
7. To also refrain from adding 'Well, I've known him longer than you, Missy.'
8. Not to tut. Ever.

She in turn pledges to...

1. Bring the grandchildren over more than twice a year
2. Not to wince when offered a home made Garibaldi biscuit.
3. Avoid running her finger over your surfaces and then staring at the accumulated dust
4. Take down the photos of your hysterectomy scar she posted on Facebook.
5. Not to lobby your son to have you declared criminally insane or committed to an institution
6. Take down the framed painting your granddaughter drew of you showing your hump and prolapsed bowel, that's hanging in the downstairs toilet.
7. Retrain the cockatoo not to say 'Show us your colostomy bag' every time you enter the house.
8. Not to tut. Ever.

Is your son-in-law better than *you*?

All dads want their daughters to be happy and to marry a nice young man with good prospects from a well-to-do family. You'll want to be reassured that they will be looked after, loved and given a decent housekeeping allowance to bring up your grandchildren.

Brushing aside the inherent sexism here (ie it's very offensive to suggest a man would ever not provide enough cash to buy the groceries), there is another, even more important factor in deciding if your little girl has chosen wisely: is he clearly a more impressive person than you ever were?

If he is, then there could be issues to contend with. After all, there was a time when she worshipped the ground you walked on, thought you were the best dad in the universe and drifted off to sleep in your arms whispering gently 'I love you, Daddy,' as her sweet doe eyes closed.

But that was then. Now, she's found a man who is taller, better looking, more successful and whose jokes make your wife laugh more than she ever did at yours.

Not only that, he earns more money, and dives a car that makes your old banger look like something left behind by the Russian army as they fled Afghanistan in 1988.

In short, is he perhaps *too good* for her? Just as you don't want her to marry Boris, the wonky-eyed, Cro-Magnon fairground operator, you equally want to avoid her being swept off her feet by a Prince Charming who will later turn out to be a cad. Or, worse, a rotter. Please excuse the language.

To better judge the situation, answer these questions...

1. His attitude to you is one of:
    A) Pity
    B) Grudging respect

2. You are a stalwart of your local Lions Club, while he:
    A) Has set up a foundation to save endangered turtles in West Papua.
    B) Once did a sponsored pub crawl

3. He:
    A) Comes from a good home
    B) Comes from a council-run home

4. He proposed:
    A) On his private jet during the decent into Monte Carlo
    B) When he thought your daughter was up the duff

5. Their first date was:
    A) Candlelit dinner on his yacht with fireworks and private perfor-
        mance from Lady Gaga.
    B) Sat at the table outside the gents at Wimpy.

6. His greatest gift to your daughter is:
    A) To give her the confidence to fulfill all her dreams and be an
        equal partner in their life together
    B) Novelty oven gloves and a pair of crotchless knickers he got
        from the market.

7. He spent his late teenage years:
    A) Leading a battalion on a covert mission in Helmand Province
    B) In a drug-induced coma in a Bexley Heath crack den.

8. The last fight he got into was
    A) While launching a successful hostile takeover for a rival mer-
        chant bank
    B) With a 25 stone bouncer outside Heebie Jeebies nightclub in
        Liverpool

9. He calls your daughter:
    A) Three times a day to express his love
    B) One of the best babes he's shagged

10. He instills in his children a sense of:
    A) Responsibility for their actions
    B) Fear of another thrashing for moving Daddy's bong.

Mostly As
You are no longer the Lion King. In fact you're a pussy compared to
your majestic son-in-law. Your only 'hope' is that he too comes to the
conclusion that he is superior to your family and falls in love with a
European royal instead.

Mostly Bs

He's not better than you, although he might be on a par. At least you'll still be able to feel smug that you're the leader of your pride, and that your daughter will continue to look up to you and, as the years pass, wish her husband was a bit more like you.

Should you tell your daughter-in-law she's a hopeless mum?

There are two considerations here. Firstly establishing that she definitely *is* a bad mother, and, secondly, deciding how much you value your relationship.

Maybe a third factor is working out how deliciously evil you want to be to this wretched cow.

On the first point, it's worth taking a few steps backwards (avoiding the dog as you do so). Yes, she may do things differently, and yes, there may have been a few hiccups and near-fatalities, but is she really *that* bad?

Well, probably yes.

In which case you need to devise a clever strategy, as blundering in and telling her she has the mothering skills of an earthworm* might not resolve the situation satisfactorily for all parties.

Instead, you can subtly destroy her confidence by innocently making 'helpful' comments that are in no way meant to be criticisms, just observations.

If you're lucky, she will have no inkling of the contempt you hold her in, and will slowly develop into a better mum. And for 'better', read 'more like you'. And that can't be a bad thing, can it? Unless *you* were a bad mum. But even if you were, you probably never realized it.

Maybe she'll even thank you, though let's not get too carried away yet.

To start off, try a few of these very reasonable asides to let her see that you are trying to help, and mean very little harm.

* Technically earthworms are hermaphrodites, so are bad mothers *and* fathers. Although evidently not *that* bad, as there are several trillion of them who all somehow survived their childhoods.

Yes, I remember how difficult it was to get *my* babies to drink formula milk. Have you thought about adding a drop of water to the powder?

I don't think that cough means he has a cold coming on, I think he just copped a plume of smoke from your Benson & Hedges.

Oh look, there's a nice Pixar film starting on the other channel. Don't worry, we can always explain what happens at the end of Saw III to little Charlotte.

No, I'm not saying they've been allowed to stay up too long, it's just that school starts in four hours.

She looks pretty as a picture! And I think her nursery friends will agree she'd be just as lovely *without* the push-up bra.

Things have certainly changed since my day. I don't think I had my first serving of KFC nuggets until *after* I was weaned.

Oh my, you're right, she does have a firm grip, doesn't she? It's just that I'm not sure it's strong enough for her to hang onto your shirt while she's on the back of the Harley.

You *are* brave doing a bungee jump while nine months pregnant. Do you think you should give me your spliff to hold while you do it?

I'm only suggesting that if she's been missing in the sea for four hours, I might have skipped the pedicure to help with the search.

No, I think the test she's sitting today at school is a GCSE, not a LGBT.

Being able to take your son to work is so special, but you're a mortician, dear.

She will soon get the idea, and you can luxuriate in the smugness that superiority brings. And, with any luck, she won't even tell your son that you've been sniping.

The result will be children who grow up in the bosom of a loving family, and get to visit their mother in the nut house every other Sunday.

What if you fall out with your grandchildren?

Yes, all this talk about conflict between generations hasn't taken into account that said conflict might stretch for several generations. If there is an age gap of more than fifty years then either a) There is potential for miscommunication, or b) There is potential for Hugh Heffner to find a new wife.

And, if you upset the grandchildren, you could also lose any contact with your children who will be forced to take sides. And, unless you have either a very strong argument on your side, or a revolver in your hand, they aren't going to take yours. Ungrateful brats.

So we need to look at ways of making sure your relationship is more akin to Red Riding Hood and her granny, rather than Granny and the wolf.

So, what are the potential areas of disagreement? Let's consider a few...

Area of conflict: You think they are obnoxious little tearaways who show no respect, have a blatant disregard for authority and will end up dead from an overdose or shot during a botched bank robbery

Solution: Wait until after their second birthday and see if they improve.

Area of conflict: They are spoilt, and have too many toys
Solution: Give them boring presents they will hate like socks, jocks or Leona Lewis albums.

Area of conflict: You suspect that they are taking drugs, but they deny it
Solution: Try selling them some of *your* drugs to catch them out

Area of conflict: They have shot your tabby with a slingshot
Solution: Make them pay a couple of bucks towards the replacement cat

Area of conflict: They haven't visited Grandpa in the palliative care ward
Solution: Suggest it won't be long before Grandpa has the opportunity to haunt them

Areas of conflict: They don't agree with your politics
Solution: Say you'll look again at the parts of Mein Kampf you may have missed the first time

Area of conflict: They slurp their food
Solution: Provide straws

Area of conflict: A police mug shot of a murder suspect looks just like your grandson
Solution: Indonesian plastic surgery clinic

Area of conflict: You are concerned they are not using contraceptive
Solution: Get Grandad to demonstrate the rhythm method

Area of conflict: They are standing on your foot
Solution: Ask them politely to move their foot

Easy! Every possible source of bad feeling suddenly vanquished. If only it was as simple to placate old club-footed Mildred next door.

Now you and your descendents can live in perfect harmony and understand each other's little quirks. Or pretend you do, whatever works.

11

When grandparents get old and doddery

"My grandmother started walking five miles a day when she was sixty. She's ninety-seven now, and we don't know where the hell she is."
Ellen Degeneres

"A stockbroker urged me to buy a stock that would triple its value every year. I told him, 'At my age, I don't even buy green bananas'."
Claude Pepper

If you chose to buy the large print version of this book, then you're already at an advantage because, at your age, small letters can be very hard to read. So I'll type very slowly to help you keep up.

This chapter is about what happens to grandparents when they are, how shall I put it, noticing that they are a bit more forgetful, and that some everyday tasks are becoming more difficult.

In short, they are losing their minds. Sorry, but old people like you appreciate directness. You're going mad, dear!

Or are you? Maybe you just forgot that you aren't going mad? Or remembered that you'd forgotten to remember that you had, in fact, forgotten that you hadn't remembered to forget that you remembered that you had forgotten.

Before we go on much further, let's address the elephant in the room. Not literally stick an address label on it, but acknowledge that advancing years are never a good thing. Except in cheese making and bonsai. Watching your body gradually shutting down and ceasing to function properly isn't fun. Especially if your mind is as sharp as ever and you feel trapped in a useless body that is fit for no purpose. At least you know how Joan Rivers feels.

We need to establish what stage of terminal decline you have reached. Then we'll consider what (if anything) we can do so that the time you have left is happy, peaceful and strait jacket-free.

Are you losing your mind?

Ok, are we ready? You need to start with question 1, and... I said **start with question 1!** And then work your way through. If you get in a muddle, look to see what question you did last and then do the one after it. No, I didn't say 'laugh at it', I... Oh, just give it a go and I'll go fetch your teeth.

1. Do you remember why you're doing this quiz?
   A Well yes, er, no...not really
   B What quiz?

2. Are you sometimes forgetful?
   A Sorry, dear, what was that?
   B I've forgotten the question

3. What's the last thing you remember?
   A Breakfast
   B Gary Cooper in *Distant Drums*

4. What sort of notes does your husband or wife leave around the house for you?

A   Buy milk

B   Socks before shoes

5. What is the capital of New Zealand?
    A   Ooh, is it a bagel?
    B   I need the toilet again, nurse

6. Did you answer question 3?
    A   Is it Humphrey Bogart?
    B   Who *are* you? Are you my son?

Mostly As

There's a chance that your brain isn't as finely tuned as it was. You have a small window of opportunity before you become an embarrassment to your family and end up in a home thinking you're the Lone Ranger.

Mostly Bs

Don't worry, you go back to bed and I'll get your medication.

I hope that puts your mind at rest, and shows that there's some life in the old girl/boy yet. If it's any consolation, the brain actually starts to decline at the age of forty-five, so, if you've got this far and not noticed, then maybe you never will. The great thing about losing your marbles is that you mostly don't know they are lost. And your grandchildren will have heaps of fun when you ask them the same question several times and call them by their parent's name. Finally you're entertaining to them. Right up until you lose bladder control.

Now, some might be reading this thinking that it's in very poor taste and mocks what is a very serious disease. It's a valid point to raise, and deserves an equally serious answer. And that is: You don't have to worry! If an oldie is losing it, they can hardly get offended, can they?

I'm glad we've addressed that, though, because the last thing I want to do is offend anyone who might be flicking through this in a bookshop and is genuinely horrified that anyone could make light of dementia. If that's you, turn to another page quickly and forget you ever read this.

If, however, you've already bought the book (and hopefully creased a few pages by now so it can't be returned) then it's less of a concern.

Granny flat horrors

What could be better than living next door to your son or daughter, still having your independence and getting to see those loveable grand-kids every single day?

Lots.

This living arrangement is to be avoided until you are on the brink of being plonked in a run-down nursing home downwind from the sewage treatment plant against your wishes. And, even then, the home option might still be better.

A granny flat is essentially a cramped bedsit into which you have to cram a life's worth of belongings while your child lives next door with his wife and kids in a palatial abode with enough space for several tennis courts.

Your kitchen will have an old hob, wobbly table and several mice, while theirs will be a bespoke designer number with an Aga, plasma TV and Smeg fridge.

While you sit in front of your fuzzy 18" TV, rotating the broken aerial on top to get Midsomer Murders, they will have a separate cinema room with projector, drinks cabinet and seating for eighteen.

If on the infrequent occasions when the interconnecting door between the properties isn't locked from their side, you pop in to borrow some tea bags, your daughter-in-law will greet you with a look of revulsion, and utter something like: 'Oh, Ethel, it's you again. Look, I don't want to be rude but my bridge club is due over in five minutes. I'll send Tom over to see you in a few days. Now where's the key to that door...'

On the *frequent* occasions, when you are required to babysit, you will be expected to drop everything at a moment's notice in return for some instant Nescafe and Digestive crumbs.

At times, days will pass when you see nothing of your 'family', but hear the sounds of laughter and merriment through the walls, and see the crates of Dom Perignon put out in the recycling bin next to your tins of Co Op own brand baked beans.

As you huddle in front of the one bar heater eating packet soup in the winter, they will lounge round their original Regency fireplace, playing board games waiting for their roast dinner to cook.

If this sounds like a bleak, even Dickensian scenario, then that's because it is. You are the Fagin to their kind-parents-who-take-Oliver-in-at-the-end; the Bob Cratchit to their Ebenezer Scrooge. And, if I'd read more of his books, I'm sure there are other, equally nonsensical, comparisons to be had.

Ok, so granny flats have one or two drawbacks. If we're ruling that option out, then what? Stay in your home? Is that possible, given your frailty?

Let's think about it. You are probably in the home where you bought up all your children. It has special memories that can never be erased from your mind (or erased from the shed in the case of the penis and balls drawing). Then again, is it too big now with just the two of you rattling around inside?

Here are the facts to consider:

Should I stay, or should I go?

Go: You don't need all those bedrooms any more
Stay: You could sublet to asylum seekers

Stay: Your family can still stay with you when they visit
Go: Oh God, the family will still stay with me if I don't get out

Stay: I'll never fit all my keepsakes and souvenirs into a smaller home
Go: I'm so old that I've forgotten about most of them anyway

Go: The garden's getting a bit much for us to manage on our own
Stay: But if you sell, the new owner's bound to notice the cannabis plantation and crystal meth lab in the shed.

Go: I'll meet lots of people my own age in sheltered accommodation
Stay: I mainly hate the elderly because they smell.

Stay: My grandchildren won't visit if I only have a small bedroom in which to entertain them
Go: Wait a sec – I don't think they've ever visited me anyway

Go: When we sell the house it'll give us a nice little nest egg to spend in our golden years...
Stay: ..until our son becomes a trustee of our estate and ring-fences it for his loft conversion

Go: We can sell up, and cruise around the world for a year!
Stay: ...and spend *12 months* in each other's company??

Stay: We'll be able to continue picking the grandchildren up from school, looking after them, babysitting in the evenings, darning all their school uniforms and having all that quality time with them.
Go: There's an old people's home with a lovely room just right for us and it's conveniently situated on the Isle of Man.

Go: If we leave it much longer, we'll be too old to move
Stay:... so someone else will end up doing the heavy lifting

How not to get dumped in a home

That's all very well, but what if it's not *you* who is deciding. What if that daughter-in-law who's always hated you has sneakily convinced her husband that you are no longer capable of making decisions for yourself? And what if a judge agrees, and you are suddenly informed that you are being moved to Shady Pines Retirement Village?

Don't sit there being so smug and assuming it won't happen. Next time the doorbell goes it'll probably be the removalists.

You need to take action now to prove that you are still reasonably compos mentis.

When your doctor is asked to make an assessment as to your state of mind, he will ask confusing, trick questions like:

1. What is your name?
2. Do you know where you are?
3. How many children do you have?
4. Who is the Prime Minister?
5. Is the Pope Catholic?

A moment's hesitation, and you're turfed out of your home and into a home. And a home isn't as good as a home.

To avoid this, scribble the answers to these five questions onto your forearm. If you're worried that they might wash off, simply don't wash.

If you start to smell, you *will* need to wash, so visit a reputable tattooist and have them permanently inked in place. And then, every time you see a doctor, urgently rattle off the answers at him: 'Barbara Snodworthy, Newcastle, three, that annoying chap, yes'.

He will smile kindly and leave you in peace. You have won a reprieve for another few months. But beware – these days not all doctors dress in white coats or wear surgical masks. You might be visited by one disguised as a normal member of society. So, just in case, rattle off the answers to anyone who approaches you, male or female (women can also disguise themselves as someone disguising themselves as a normal member of society).

Ok, we've established that your mind is possibly still intact. But what about your body? That's certainly seen better days. Are you aware of just what a state of disrepair it is in, or still in denial?

To be fair, there may be no need to panic at this stage. There's a small chance you could be fine. Let's work out a checklist and go through the main areas of concern one by one...

Then you can panic.

Are you blind?
1. Can you read this?
    A) Yes
    B) No

Mostly As
You're not blind. Not yet, anyway.

Mostly Bs
Liar! You just read it. There's a phrase for folk like you: 'people who pretend to be blind'.

Are you deaf?
1. Do you have trouble hearing people on the phone?
    A) Yes. But there's a chance I was talking into a banana by mistake
    B) No. Because no one ever rings me anyway. Or maybe they do.

2. Did you hear the intercity train before it hit your car?
   A) Oh yes, very clearly, but I thought I was watching *Brief Encounter*
   B) No, but I didn't have my glasses on

3. Do you have to turn the volume on the TV up all the way?
   A) Only if I see The Queen's on.
   B) Pardon, dear, I can't hear you over the TV, which I've had to turn up all the way.

Mostly As
You're not deaf, you're just a bit confused.

Mostly Bs
You're not deaf either, and when you are, you'll be too far gone to care.

Are you incontinent?
1. Is there a damp stain on the carpet where you are standing
   A) Ooh yes, but the dog's licked most of it up.
   B) Yes, but it's probably raining

2. Has your doctor ever told you that you're incontinent?
   A) No, I've never been to mainland Europe
   B) Yes, but I thought he was taking the piss

3. Do you wear a nappy at night?
   A) Yes, and it's the size of a watermelon by morning
   B) Yes, but it's more a fetish thing

4. If you get a bit overexcited watching the footy, what do you chant
   A) Up the Arsenal!
   B) Surf's up!

Mostly As

I'm afraid your pelvic floor muscles aren't what they used to be. Well, they are technically still pelvic floor muscles, but they no longer protect the floor.

Mostly Bs

That urine smell can no longer be passed off as asparagus soup. And the cork isn't really working.

Are you bald?

1. Does it take you a bit longer to wash your face each morning?
    A) Yes
    B) No

2. Have you been getting through flannels at an increasing rate?
    A) Yes
    B) No

3. Is there more hair in your nose and ears than on your head?
    A) Yes
    B) No

4. Are you, in fact, bald?
    A) Yes, but I assumed I was having chemo
    B) No, but I think I have less pubic hair

Mostly As

Yes, you are a slap head. And a stupid one at that for not realizing sooner.

Mostly Bs

You're either the proud owner of a full head of hair, or you're Elton John.

Are you getting a bit stooped?
1. Looking straight ahead, what can you see?
    A) The horizon
    B) My feet

Mostly As
You are not stooped

Mostly Bs
You are stooped

Are you in a coma?
1. Are your close family gathered by your bedside?
    A) Yes, bless them...hey, did one of you just turn off my life support? I'm not dead yet. Oh, now I am.
    B) No, but to be fair it's the cup final today.

2. Can you see a light at the end of a tunnel?
    A) Yes..and...and...is that you, Pops?
    B) No, just utter blackness

3. Does your brain feel like it's dead?
    A) No more than usual
    B) The doctor just removed it for medical research, so I'm not sure

Mostly As
I'm afraid it's not looking good. On the positive side, at least you're not in pain. Except for that irritating itch on your nose.

Mostly Bs

It's possible you're just in a deep sleep. You'll probably come to in about 2016

Are you dead?

1. Can you detect a pulse?
   A) Yes, I think it's a chickpea
   B) Yes, oh wait…no

2. Where are you right now?
   A) In some sort of Hell with pale looking, dead people
   B) In a nice silky bed, with a wooden lid.

3. What is the last thing you remember?
   A) A rancid, sick taste in my mouth, life being sucked out of me
   B) A black fin, and lots of teeth

Mostly As

Relax, you're merely in a vegetarian restaurant.

Mostly Bs

I'm afraid you're dead. Still, at least you're not in a vegetarian restaurant.

Medical prognosis

Through these series of tests, we've scientifically proven that you are older than you used to be. You can put your pants back on now.

But being old is OK - kids these day don't want their grandparents to be too young or it means their mother gave birth when she was twelve. A bit of crumbliness is a good thing, as long as bits of you don't crumble off into their non-fat lattes.

Whatever your health, just be thankful you have a loving family. A family who will be there for you in case of emergency and maybe even buy you one of those personal alarms that you can press if you have a fall. Though if it's linked to the local real estate agent for him to rush over and value the house, there's a chance they're not quite as loving as you had first thought.

How long should you live?

Until twenty years ago, all grandparents were either decrepit, or dead. There was no in between. Our seniors did 'old people things' like knitting, lawn bowls or having strokes.

These days, old people aren't even old any more. Seventy used to be ancient, now most of AC/DC are nearly there.

The human race has evolved. Women have their kids later in life, the retirement age keeps going up, and no one dies of old age until they are at least 110.

It's now possible to be retired for longer than you actually worked. Which is a good thing – except when you have to invite your grandparents to your retirement party.

Kids now have grandparents and great grandparents. And even great, great grandparents, if we include cryogenically frozen heads. In fact your grandchildren may be grandparents themselves.

Our seniors aren't behaving like seniors did fifty years ago. No, they have developed new patterns of behaviour. In short, they are acting younger. Sometimes much younger.

The idea of an eighty-year-old owning a mobile phone and ordering her groceries from Lidl online would have been unthinkable just fifteen years ago*. A child visiting his grandmother might expect her to be busily making fresh lemonade or crocheting. Imagine the shock if he turns up to find her playing Halo 2 on her X Box. Especially with those arthritic fingers.

Even the age at which you get old has changed. There was a time when forty would have been considered ancient. In Neanderthal circles, you learned to walk erect, went in search of fire, ate a sabre-toothed tiger, did a bit of sexual intercourse and then had the decency to die before you became a burden.

But since then, the average life expectancy has crept up and up as we gradually cure death. Now not even three score years and ten is enough Oh no, our septuagenarians want to be octogenarians, and when they manage that, they then aspire to become nonagenarians.

Which is all very well until gangs of centenarians start roaming the streets trying to find the collective noun for people who live past 110**.

And where will it stop? Will our grandchildren live to be 120, 130 or will even that age soon be considered passé when the first human reaches 150? And where are we going to get all those extra candles from?

There are already seven billion people on the planet, and soon it'll be eight billion. If that wasn't scary enough, think of eight billion people all living past 100, and all of them being grumpy old sods. It's like some apocalyptic nightmare of the undead.

Will we have to colonize other planets to fit everyone in? Will the retirement age have to be raised to ninety? And if they all have free travel cards, where are we going to find another billion buses?

There's also the issue of whether people really *want* to live that long. If you are technically elderly for more than half your lifespan, then that's a long time to put up with rheumatism and surgical supports.

Luckily, Mother Nature has found a cunning way to keep us in check: pies. And chips.

Our path towards immortality has been stopped in its tracks by morbid obesity. We are now too fat to become old, as our hearts haven't yet caught up to our stomachs. In fact, if current trends continue, few of us will make it past fifty.

Which will have far reaching consequences. Will biscuit tins in nursing homes have to be fitted with rape alarms to keep off the angry (and hungry) hoards? Will Macca's launch a specially liquidized McOldie burger? Will we be glued to The Biggest Gainer on TV? Will all babies be fitted with a gastric band at birth?

Anyway, the point is we were all living too long, so something had to give***.

But that still leaves us with many more years on our hands. And a feeling that even when we nudge sixty, we're not really *old* old. Well, we are in terms of years, but not in our mindset.

So when grandchildren come along, we're not all going to fit the cliché of a pensioner. Just as parents can be young and hip, so can grandparents. Perhaps we need to work out just how 'down with the kids' you are.

* Partly because Lidl online didn't exist. They were the days when the Internet was clearly not going to catch on.
** Turns out it's 'Supercenterarian' and there are about three hundred of them lose on the planet.
*** our elasticated waistbands

Are you a funky crumbly?
1.   What are you planning this weekend
     A) A hip hop party
     B) A hip op

2.   Your music collection…
     A) Contains Beyonce, Adele and Katy Perry
     B) Is stored on wax cylinders

3.   The last time you hit the dance floor…
     A) You pulled a man forty years your junior
     B) You pulled your groin

4.   The last time you had sex..
     A) …you were nearly busted by the grandkids
     B) You nearly busted your varicose veins

5. You communicate with most of your friends through
   A) Twitter or Facebook
   B) A ouija board

6. If the two of you are alone, you might...
   A) Have a sneaky joint
   B) Put out one of your joints

7. LGBT stands for
   A) Lesbian, gay, bisexual, transgender
   B) Let grannies be tetchy

Mainly As
You are aged, but still sharp. The advancing years have been kind to your grey matter. It's just a pity that your body gave up the ghost years ago.

Mostly Bs
You are still baffled by much of the 20th Century, let alone the 21st. Times have moved on, but you've stayed still. Possibly because you're too heavy for anyone to push your wheelchair. There are barbary apes more tech savvy than you.

Deciding on your last words
The term 'famous last words' has precious little to do with the actual last words of the famous. But there have, in fact, been lots of famous last words uttered by the famous. And it's unlikely that the more pithy ones were dreamt up on the spot. No, they were planned well in advance as, while you're in the process of dying, the words most likely to come to mind will be things like:

1. 'Aaaaaaagh, oh God, nooooo...'
2. 'Nurse, I think I've followed throu...'

3. 'The one thought I'd like to leave you with is…er.. give me a minute. Something like….(gurgle, gurgle)….'
4. No, idiot, the live wire is….'
5. We'll be safe from the lightning under this nice, big pine tr….'
6. Ha! I'll bet it's not even loaded

No one's going to put any of those in a dictionary of quotations. You need something either profound, unique, witty or bizarre. Like the final words of these celebrities…

"Go on – get out. Last words are for fools who haven't said enough."

Karl Marx

"Either this wallpaper goes or I do"

Oscar Wilde

"I know you've come to kill me. Shoot, coward, you are only going to kill a man."

Che Guevara

"Kiss me, Hardy"

Admiral Nelson

"I do not believe in my death"

Salvadore Dali

"I told you I was ill"

Spike Milligan

"I should never have switched from Scotch to Martinis."

Humphrey Bogart

"Don't worry, they usually don't swim backwards"

Steve Irwin

And make sure whatever you come up with isn't too long, or else there's a risk of not making it to the end of the sentence.

For example if you're planning to say: 'There is one thing which might surprise you - I am not a man who holds grudges, I am a man of honour' there's a danger all you'll manage is: 'There is one thing which might surprise you – I am not a man'.

If you really can't think of anything, you could use the opportunity to play one last joke on your children or grandchildren

When you feel your pulse weakening, say things like:

"Is that you Santa? I'm coming now"
"Why, St Peter, is it No Pants Day in Heaven?"
"And I left the winning lottery ticket in the..."
"Whoa! I'm going stiff already, and it's not rigor mortis, fnar fnar"
"Rosebud"

Should you bequeath stuff to your grandchildren?

Making a will should be easy enough, but the advent of grandchildren makes things complicated. Yes, you can divide your estate up evenly between your kids and leave it up to them to decide if any of *their* children deserve anything.

Then again, are your offspring really the best people to make such important decisions? Possibly not.

But I'm assuming that you possess things that other people will want to actually have. You may cherish the brass plate presented to Great Aunt June for her work as an embalmer in the Boar War, but your kids will probably use it as a doorstop or ashtray.

And the gold locket you've worn for sixty years containing hair snipped from your grandfather's chest as he set off for Flanders will probably be taken to the pawn shop before your body is even cold.

So we need to establish which of your belongings have great sentimental value, and which have an actual value. The latter will be easy to identify - they are the items your children have already singled out and admired in the hope that they will be left to them.

When you try to explain the story behind the little clay pot you were given by your grandmother as a child, they will respond: 'Yeah, yeah, great, but that Lalique glass sculpture next to it would be simply perfect for our conservatory.'

Another common tactic is to play on your emotions: 'You know, Grandma, you are so special to me. I will tell my children one day just how lucky I was to have you. In fact when we have your original Picasso pencil drawing in our living room, it'll mean that you're never forgotten.'

Others might not be so coy: 'Mum, can I have your 17th Century writing desk when you're dead? Yeah? Good, now get your coat on and we'll go alter your will.'

Such behaviour can be very upsetting. It's not pleasant thinking of your nearest and dearest scavenging through your cupboards and drawers the moment you pass away to see what they can plunder.*

But you can fight back, and maybe teach them a lesson or two. If you got through the Alzheimer's quiz unscathed, then you are still of sound mind and can still dictate what goes in your will. Obviously, as grandparents, you'll leave everything to your husband/wife, so this is really if you are a widow(er). In which case, please accept condolences for your loss, but I'm sure you'll agree it was worth it when you see the plan**.

* Although the concept would make a great reality TV show. 'The Ex-Granny Factor', or 'Where There's a Will, There's a Way'. Or something
** Or *feel* it using Braille if you failed the blindness test

The last will and testament of.............. (your name)

I, ...(your name again, obviously), being of sound and disposing mind hereby make, publish and declare the following to be my last Will and Testament, revoking all previous wills made by me.

I direct that my estate, through my appointed executor will be distributed as follows.

1. Following my death, I would like seven days of official mourning and fasting. Anyone in breach of this order shall forsake any further claim to my possessions.
2. My property and its contents are bequeathed to the Toowoomba Donkey Sanctuary so that they may continue their important work.
3. My Chihuahua, Minxy, I leave to my dear daughter, Julie in the hope it helps cure her severe dog allergy
4. My 200-year-old Persian rug in which so many of my family have kindly expressed an interest, is to be divided between my four children. In fact as you read this, old Mr Franks, the gardener is carefully doing the dividing with his chainsaw.
5. My lay-about brother, Charlie badgered me for years to be mentioned in my will. So hi Charlie!
6. To my lovely daughters-in-law, Becky and Grace, who live such busy lives that they could never visit, I leave my set of Le Creuset pans. However, they must mud wrestle for them in the presence of my solicitor and a representative of the local paper.

7. All my jewellery is, in fact, fake. I sold the real stuff years ago to fund my heroin addiction. Consequently, the only silver we have left are spoons.

8. Now I am departed, I feel a solemn duty to reveal a few family secrets which I have kept all these years:

    i)   Anna – your pet rabbit didn't run away to the wild when you were six, he was savagely ripped to pieces and eaten by the neighbour's Rottweiler.

    ii)   John – your father is actually old Mr Franks, but let him finish the rug before saying anything

    iii) Becky – my son cheated on you with an obese Russian flight attendant and Mad Brenda from Argos.

    iv)   Your Grandfather Johnny didn't die saving his battalion in WWII, he was Hitler's personal proctologist.

    v)   My favourite child was always Peter, and my least favourite Julie.

    vi)   John – your children are quite revolting. Not only are they ugly, but they smell and one of them is developing a grotesque bunion.

    vii) Anna – your son, Luke, is gay and banging his geography teacher, Mr Harris.

As you were of sound mind when you prepared this, there will be nothing they can do about it. The only shame is that you won't be there to witness the anger and gnashing of teeth. Unless you fake your own death.

One small tip here is to keep the will secret while you're still alive to avoid any unnecessarily spilt blood. After all, you don't want to ruin the surprise.

12

When grandparents go all evil

"My grandmother was a very tough woman. She buried three husbands and two of them were just napping."

Rita Rudner

"Good old grandsire ... we shall be joyful of thy company."

William Shakespeare

So far we've established that being a grandparent means putting up with a lot of stress, mainly caused by your younger generations. Hopefully you now feel better able to cope with this, and not let it completely devastate your life.

If you have, then you'll need to recommend this book to at least two hundred of your closest friends before you even finish reading this sentence so that other people like you will feel the benefit.

All done?

Ok, well, I'll pause for a few seconds while you get on with it.

Great. They will thank you for it when they get their lives back, or blame you forever for wrecking whatever relationship they formerly had with their family.

Either way, there's one thing we haven't yet considered, something that has probably never crossed either *your* mind, nor the minds of your grandchildren.

What happens when it's the *grandparent* who is the problem? And, more than that, how does a family cope when their seniors aren't particularly nice?

Of course the Catholics reckon everyone is born evil* in which case it shouldn't surprise them when some of that evilness is still lurking fifty years later.

After all, just because you're old, doesn't mean that you're immune from committing the odd atrocity. In fact most despotic world leaders are a tad long in the tooth, and just look at all the wars, famines, genocides and petty arguments they've caused.

In most dictatorships, the leader goes on leading well into his dotage, irrespective of how many 'senior moments' he has a day. Ronald Reagan and Boris Yeltsin had the beginnings of Alzheimer's when they were both still president, and no one seemed to care much.

But being a bit mad isn't the same as being a bit bad**. And there have certainly been some mightily badass old folk in the history of the world. In fact there have probably been more nasty, bloodthirsty people *over* fifty than under.

So is the unavoidable conclusion that *all* old people are evil? Maybe even the ones who *seem* all meek and mild might really be harbouring murderous thoughts and would act them out if only they could manage to stand up.

Would the world be a better place if life expectancy were still thirty-five and there were no nefarious wrinklies wreaking havoc?

Of course not – for a start, cruise companies wouldn't be able to stay afloat*** without all the grey nomads. So old people do fulfill some sort of purpose.

And maybe the evil ones do too. Maybe, if we examined a few well known psychotic grandparents, we could learn some valuable life lessons ourselves.

* Well, full of sin anyway. And sin is evil, isn't it?

** This isn't 'bad' the way Michael Jackson used it to mean 'good'. This bad is really bad, and bad's not good.

*** This wasn't a deliberate pun as it would have been a bit lame. However, if you chortled, it was a deliberate pun

What can we learn from criminally insane grandparents?

One of the most important rules in life is that you must learn from your mistakes. You look at where you went wrong, examine the error of judgment and hopefully don't make it a second time.

Indeed, some scholars say that the more mistakes, the better, as each one will make you a wiser person. However, a mistake is only good if you *do* learn from it. If you don't (or even choose not to), then you're in dangerous territory.

If you don't care who you hurt, or what damage you do, then you will almost certainly end up like one of these particularly wicked grandparents.

Evil grandparent: Osama Bin Laden, giver and taker of life

If nothing else, Bin Laden was a good father. Or rather a prolific one, siring between twenty and twenty-six kids with his five wives. The number of grandchildren is unknown, but is probably over thirty, in which case no wonder he was hiding for so many years. Christmases and birthdays alone would have decimated his fortune, which was estimated to be about £30 million.*

Just like Terry Wogan, Osama has saddled his grandkids with a famous surname that will be hard to live up to. Unlike Terry, however, he had to flee his native country after the CIA put a £25 million bounty on his head**.

Most evil act: Using one of his wives as a human shield when he was finally cornered. Two would have worked better.

Grandparenting method: Moral guidance delivered from afar, usually on a video tape sent to al-Jazeera.

* And we all know that sneaky non-Christian kids still expect a Christmas stocking.
** The only thing on the Wogan head is a £25 wig

Evil grandparent: 'Grandma', an 82-year-old hooker
Police in the Taiwanese city of Taipei have arrested a woman known only as 'Grandma' several times. The octogenarian granny is thought to be the world's oldest prostitute, not so much walking the streets as shuffling along them.

While most grandparents are content to lazily draw their pension and spend most of it on the slot machines, Grandma is much more conscientious and an astute business woman, showing her market knowledge by charging a tenth of what the younger girls get paid. And grandchildren like nothing more than a grandparent they can look up to and respect for not letting advancing years stop her being the oldest professional doing the oldest profession.

Most evil act: Not turning the lights out for her clients
Grandparenting style: Grandchildren must join the queue like anyone else.

Evil grandparent: Bernie Madoff, jailed investor who made off with £50 billion
Too few grandparents think hard enough about providing for their children and grandchildren. Retiring to a warden controlled unit up the coast is all very well if you're happy to let your children struggle to make ends meet and risk them falling into poverty. Such fears led New Yorker Bernie to create a fail-safe Ponzi scheme to make sure *his* family would be fabulously wealthy for generations to come while all the clients he ripped off lost everything. And if it wasn't for those

meddling kids at the tax office, he'd have gotten away with it. But, with good behaviour, he'll be a free man when he turns 201.

Most evil act: Attempting suicide on Christmas Eve. Poor Santa would have been distraught, even though, arguably, Bernie hadn't been such a good boy that year.

Grandparenting style: Advice on investing pocket money to be taken with a pinch of salt.

Evil grandparent: Phil Spector, actress-shooting record producer

Just one little cold blooded murder, and the whole world forgets all those classic hits by The Ronettes, Righteous Brothers and lots of other irritating 60s bands. Phil generously fathered kids with two wives and might have done with a third had he not been jailed for nineteen years for gunning down an actress lured back to his pad. Clues to his evilness were there for all to see, however, especially in his choice of wigs. Nothing shows a grand jury that you're taking proceedings seriously like a giant Hair Bear Bunch hairpiece.

Most evil act: Producing Da Doo Ron Ron for The Crystals

Grandparenting style: Gets a bit disgruntled if screaming babies don't produce wall of sound

Evil grandparent: Dorothea Puente, serial killing landlady

White-haired little old lady Dorothea ran a lovely boarding house in Sacramento, California for the elderly. So devoted to them was she, that she even offered to go and pick up their welfare money. Now, we all know how disrespectful and annoying tenants can be, and doting Nanna Dorothea had just the answer – she killed them and buried the bodies in her basement if they got wise to the fact she was stealing all their cash. Seven corpses were found, and she was suspected of killing two others.

Most evil act: Brought out a recipe book in jail called *Cooking with a Serial Killer*

Grandparenting style: Gets a bit testy if there's not enough cash in your money box.

Evil grandparents: Ray and Faye Copeland, Bonnie and Clyde with wrinkles

This husband and wife had the honour of becoming the oldest ever couple sentenced to death in the US when they were 73 and 69 respectively. Their so-called crime? Killing up to twelve hobos who worked on their farm and outgrew their usefulness. As Ray already had a conviction for buying cattle at auction with dud cheques, he instead signed up any vagrants who passed by his ranch in Mooresville, Missouri to buy the cows for him. They then disappeared without trace. The hobos, that is, not the cows. The cattle themselves probably didn't suspect what was going on.

Most evil act: Mass genocide (of beef cattle)

Grandparenting style: Enjoyed games with buckets and spades, but the two-metre long holes were often filled in unexpectedly, thus spoiling the fun.

Evil grandparent: Granny Goodness, tubby comic book supervillain

Though arguably not actually real, Granny Goodness is an excellent example of what happens when our most senior members of society get ratty. For the inappropriately named Goodness, animated star of The Justice League, Superman and loads of other DC comics, it all started when, as a young girl, she was asked to slaughter her beloved dog by her army trainer. As a doting animal lover, she refused and killed the trainer instead, thereby kicking off decades of badness, including trying to destroy Earth with a comet, murdering Supergirl and using her superpowers to kill anyone who got in her way.

Most evil act: In one comic adventure, Wonder Woman tragically sacrifices her own life to kill her. And that meant no more tight blue undies and long, long legs. Shame on you, Granny, you went too far that time.

Grandparenting style: Slight risk she'd train grandchildren to be warriors and join her in her quest to destroy civilization. Unlikely to bake cupcakes with them.

Evil grandparent: Betty Neumar, multiple husband killer
Divorces can be messy things. All that paperwork, solicitor's fees, working out who gets the worm farm and listening to your mother saying that she always knew this would happen.

This considerate US lady decided to avoid all these unpleasantries by simply killing her five husbands when they got on her nerves. Of course, she had the good sense to make sure they had life insurance first, obviously thinking about her grandchildren's inheritance. Moving from Ohio to New York and then Florida, she dispatched her men by variously hiring hitmen, blasting them with shotguns and poisoning.

Most evil act: Dying in hospital before she could be sentenced to death

Grandparenting style: Stressing the importance to a growing child of having a variety of grandpas to help nurture them.

Evil grandparents: Helen Golay and Olga Rutterschmidt, murderous biddies
Despite being 77 and 75 respectively, this slightly doddery Los Angeles duo killed two homeless men after taking out insurance policies worth £2.8m on them. Both men were drugged and then run over in an isolated alleyway.

They were arrested, but police had no real evidence against them…right up until the minute Olga berated Helen for getting greedy while the cops were listening in.

Most evil act: Both getting their hair dyed red. As if their family weren't embarrassed enough.

Grandparenting style: Can teach the importance of helping vagrants to get off the streets… but only up to a point.

Evil grandparent: JL Rountree, 91-year-old bankrobber

The world's oldest gun-toting grandfather walked into a bank in Abilene, Texas with an envelope, on which he had scrawled 'Robbery'. He then shuffled out with £2,000 and calmly drove away in his Buick Sentinal.

Inexplicably he didn't get far before the police caught up with him. It was actually his third bank robbery – he started young when, at just 86, he held up a branch in Biloxi, Mississippi and then followed it up a year later with another in Pensacola Florida.

However, he had the last laugh by dying after only serving a year in prison.

Most evil act: Inspiring a god-awful honky tonk swing song by Dag and the Bulleit Boys called The Ballad of JL Rountree.

Grandparenting style: Out of consideration for their feelings, waiting until his grandchildren were adults before embarrassing them.

Evil grandparent: Laura Lundquist, 98-year-old strangler

We all know that having a roomie can be tough for any number of reasons – annoying posters, snoring, body odour, group sex parties etc.

For sweet natured great-grandparent, Laura, her main bugbear was the arrangement of the beds in the nursing home in Dartmouth, Massachusetts. Hers was stuck in a corner, while 100-year-old Elizabeth Barrow's was right next to the window.

It just wasn't fair. Laura vowed that she would outlive her friend so that she could gaze at the lovely view out the window. As her eyesight wasn't great, she might as well have been gazing at a wall, but that wasn't the point.

So, one night, after checking the nurses weren't about to burst in, Laura put a plastic bag over Elizabeth's head to suffocate her and, while she was waiting, strangled her too for good measure.

Most evil act: Forgetting she'd committed the murder soon afterwards, probably to beat a lie detector. Clever.

Grandparenting style: Loving, gentle and kind, as long as her bed's in the right place.

Evil grandparent: Don Corleone, mumbling mafia mobster

All children benefit from a good godfather to teach them right from wrong, respect for their family and how to rub out those who squeal to the authorities, and Vito Corleone, the head of New York's premier crime family, was no exception. True, you could barely hear a word he said, and, yes, you did have to put up with several rival gangs trying to kill him, but at least he had all his own teeth and didn't smell of wee.

Most evil act: Embracing morbid obesity

Grandparenting style: If his granddaughter wakes up to find he's bought her a horse, she should manage her expectations about exactly how much of the horse she really has.

Evil grandparent: Vera McGrath, had husband's head on pitch-fork

Not content with beating her husband, Brian, to death, this Irish granny then held a party where his body was burnt while she danced merrily around holding his head on the end of a garden fork.

To prevent grandchild, Leon, missing out on the fun, she proudly told him how his granddady had begged for his life seconds before she killed him with an iron bar

Most evil act: The hommus dip ran out midway through the festivities

Grandparenting style: Doesn't fork out on presents, forks out on human heads.

Do *you* know an evil oldie?

Now you've read about the exploits of these largely misunderstood individuals, it's clear that old age doesn't have to mean a lack of criminality. If you're a bad 'un as a young person, why on earth should you change in your dotage?

One question, though, is how self aware these people were. Did they realize they were evil, or, in their minds, were they just living life as best they could and assuming everyone committed the odd murder here and there?

At what point do you become so psychotic that you don't realize you're psychotic?

Who knows, maybe *you* actually know a pensioner who seems quite normal, but is actually plotting their first bout of serial killing. Would you even recognise the signs?

A starting point would be to look out for a few clues like these:

- Stockpiling rat poison, but lives on the 87th floor
- Just married a man who is 108 years old and taking him to Blackpool Pleasure Beach for honeymoon
- Has cancelled subscription to *Better Homes and Gardens* in favour of *Better Serial Killing* Magazine.
- His last eight wives all died after tripping on their stairs
- Puts water in the mug before milk when making pot of tea.
- Pen pals with the Yorkshire Ripper, Bernie Madoff and Katie Price
- You're sure you found an eyelid in one of her home made sausages
- Currently knitting a pair of handcuffs
- Listens to Ozzy Osbourne albums to mask the muffled banging from cellar
- Has persuaded wealthy great aunt to do the Seven Peaks Challenge.
- You've seen them wearing a Man Utd shirt

Are *you* evil?

Before we get too carried away with *other* people doing the Devil's work, let's examine if we are indeed throwing stones in a glass house.

If you're so convinced someone else is a danger to society, then where does that leave you, eh?

Are you really all sweetness and light, or do you too harbour dark, sinister thoughts?

If you *are* evil (and it's only an 'if' at this stage), then you may well not only realize it, but be reveling in it and emitting mad, cackling laughter even now.

Or maybe you're a Jekyll and Hyde type who bakes pies for the Women's Institute by day, and murders prostitutes by night, possibly to provide filling for the pies*.

Either way, your chances of being a successful and beloved grandparent do hinge on whether you're making a habit of bumping off strangers.

Though I suppose you don't have to actually end people's lives to be evil. You could just be a *little* bit evil. Sort of 'evil-lite'. And, if that's the case, then I'd stop all this unnecessary worrying as no one is *wholly* without sin.**

To put your mind at ease, we can do a simple, yet foolproof, quiz.

1. You notice a baby badger with a broken paw. Do you:
    A) Bandage it up as best you can and give it some milk
    B) Use it as bait to catch and eat its mother

2. A malnourished little boy wearing rags comes to your door asking for food. Do you
    A) Cook him a meal and alert the police
    B) Cook him a meal and alert the police, after he's cleaned out your chimney.

3. The doll you gave to your first granddaughter was:
    A) Dressed in a cute babygro with a dummy in its mouth and a little bottle with which to feed it

B)   Anatomically correct and stolen during your last visit to the criminal psychiatrist

4.   Complete this sentence: The sins of the father…
    A)   …shall *not* be visited upon the son
    B)   …are nothing compared to the sins of this grandfather Ha, ha ha (sinister sounding belly laugh)

5.   As a child you:
    A)   May have once pulled the legs off a daddy longlegs
    B)   May have once pulled the legs off a Labradoodle.

6.   On the mantelpiece, you have a:
    A)   Framed photo of your mum and dad's wedding
    B)   Framed photo of your mum and dad's autopsy

7.   The last item of clothing you bought was:
    A)   A nice cardi you got in the BHS sale
    B)   Made from one hundred and one Dalmatian pups

Mostly As

Don't think that people aren't wise to your 'butter wouldn't melt' smile. Some might even call it 'menacing'. Or 'sinister'. Or other words from the page in the Thesaurus where you were looking up 'evil'. Like 'beastly', 'pernicious' and 'unpropitious'. Yes, and when we look up what these words mean, I think we'll find the word 'evil' somewhere in the definition.

Mostly Bs

People like you are sadly misunderstood. You'd be the first to admit that you're not perfect, but after a few innocent mistakes, suddenly people tar you with the evil brush. It's not fair. In fact it's so *un*fair that just this once, you're allowed to do something a bit nefarious.

* Technically that would make you a Sweeney Todd type rather than Jekyll and Hyde, especially if you engaged your wife to make the pies.
** Except the Duchess of Cambridge and Olivia Newton John

All your Grandparenting questions answered – guaranteed*

"How young can you die of old age?"

Steven Wright

"My grandmother is over eighty and still doesn't need glasses. Drinks right out of the bottle."

Henry Youngman

Well, we've covered pretty much every aspect of being a grandparent. If you've made it this far**, then well done. Most probably didn't, and are foraging through their wallets to see if they kept the receipt.

You are now ready to be a grandparent. And a very good one at that. It's true there may be troubles ahead, but such is life. At least you're in a better position than all your friends who've chosen to read a 'proper' book about grandparenting instead. Poor old cobbers.

So good luck, and do let me know how you get on****. Before we finish, however, we need to make sure that every query you might have has been answered. After all, all grandparents are unique so there's a small chance you might be bursting to ask a couple of supplementary questions on matters not so far addressed.

To that end, here are a few, from readers who have already written in…

* Not guaranteed
** Which you must have if you're reading this***
*** Unless you skipped the first eleven chapters. Wise move
**** if you *really* have to. Disclaimer: No letters will be opened, unless obviously containing cash.

My granddaughter is always teasing me about my blue hair rinse. What can I do?
Bertha, 71, Dorking

Cutting her out of your will is my first instinct, but that alone won't stop her taking the piss. Why not try a few more colours so she can see that, if pushed, you can be *even more* embarrassing so she should be grateful that all you're doing is sticking to the Marge Simpson look.

I'm worried that my grandson has an inner ear problem as he's so clumsy and is always falling over, but my son just brushes my fears aside.
Wally, 49, Coventry

The modern world has a solution for an issue like this…Youtube. Simply make sure that next time he visits, you place lots of objects around the house that will look hilarious when he knocks them down. Capture it all on film, he'll be an Internet sensation and you can collect £200 from sending it to a trashy TV show.

I know I had something to ask, but I can't for the life of me remember what it was.
Arthur, 83, Southampton

I'm in a real tizzy because my granddaughter, Alice won't visit me because she's allergic to my cat, the poor child. Should I put the puss in a bag and throw it in the Firth of Forth?
Rita, 51, Edinburgh

It's a thought, but a potentially better idea is to carefully try to build up Alice's immunity to animal fur. Invite her over, promising that the cat will be locked away and then, as soon as she's in the house, stuff the animal in her face for a few minutes, holding it tight in case she struggles.

After ten or twelve visits, she should start to feel the benefit.

Does anyone know how to get grass stains out of a panty girdle?
Nan, 61, Wolverhampton

I'm sure they do, but this book is about grandparents, not laundry solutions.

My eldest grandchild is doing sixteen years for people smuggling. What should I take for him when I visit?
Frank, 58, Swansea

Well, let's discount a diary or calendar. These days, prisoners are treated very differently from when you and I were banged up. The emphasis now is on rehabilitation and learning new skills so that inmates are ready for the outside world after completing their sentences. Jails have extensive libraries and workshops so there's every chance he'll have everything he needs already. Maybe just bake a cake and tuck some hardcore pornography into the middle.

Ah, I've remembered what it was now. It was about my granddaughter, I think. Give me a minute…
Arthur, 83, Southampton

In answer to the lady who has grass stains in her panty girdle, I'd suggest soaking it in a biodegradable stain remover for two hours before washing at 60 degrees.
Paula, 49, Stevenage

How come all these old folk are writing to you when the book isn't even published yet?

Ted, (age not supplied), Dundee

My daughter still puts a nappy on her son, and he's nearly seven. I'm worried he'll be bulied at school if the other children find out.
Sheila, 48, Dublin

You're right that kids can be very cruel, and finding a pull-up on a classmate (especially if soiled) can be disastrous. However, at least being remorselessly bullied might spur him to control his urination, and move on to undies. *You*, however, need to consider adult nappies, if the smell of your letter is anything to go by.

Got it! I was going to ask about which Lego set I should buy for my 13-year-old grandson
Arthur, 83, Southampton

If he's a teenager still playing with plastic bricks, then you have a much bigger problem on your hands. Shouldn't he be out shoplifting or car surfing by now? If he does insist on Lego, see if he can build you something useful like a walking stick, commode or ear trumpet.

Has anyone noticed that all young people today seem to ride round in vans solving mysteries?
Bernard, 91, Tumbridge Wells

Have you asked the nurse to change the TV channel?

My daughter, Cassandra, is forty-five and still hasn't given me grandchildren. How can I hurry her along a bit.
Wendy, 68, Solihull

There are several possible reasons for this, Wendy. Firstly, not everyone can have children. It may be that she has been trying for years without success. Another possibility is that she hasn't found Mr Right yet, or, indeed, that she is looking for a Mrs Right instead. It's best not to interfere unless a friend of yours has a gay son who wants to donate sperm.

No, wait, he's not thirteen, he's three. My finger must have slipped. And he's a girl.
Arthur, 83, Southampton

Three-year-olds are easy to buy for as they are fascinated by everything, even cardboard boxes. The best option is to buy her a Lego set suitable for a four-year-old, empty out the bricks and give her the box to play with. Then, for her next birthday, you can give her the actual set. Two presents for the price of one!

How Paula can possibly think that soaking the item of clothing in a stain remover will get rid of a grass stain is beyond me. When my Harold and I get frisky in a field, I sometimes have to soak my panty girdle in one part bleach to two parts water.
Frances, 77, Fleetwood

I'm about to become a great, great grandma, and I'm a little worried that with so many grandchildren, great grandchildren and now great, great grandchildren to see, I won't have time to visit my mother as often.
June, 103, Mansfield

It's a common problem, June. Your mum will have to get used to seeing a bit less of you, but a good solution is Skype. Get her to go to Curry's and buy herself a laptop with an integral camera. The HP Pavilion G6-1310AX notebook has 1GB of dedicated graphics, up to 2.5GHz, dual-core AMD A4 3305M accelerated processor and an impressive 4GB RAM. If she's worried about its capacity, it has an integrated 10/100BASE-T Ethernet LAN (RJ-45 connector) 802.11b/g/n WLAN. I'm sure she'll agree that will suit her just fine.

I'm not a grandparent yet, but do you have any useful advice for fathers?
Pete, 41, Stourbridge

I'm glad you asked that Pete. As it happens, the previous book in this series was all about being a dad. It's called Muddle Your Way Through Fatherhood and is available from those nice people at Amazon.com. Just try not to do anything rash before you've read it.

My seven-year-old granddaughter asked me to help her with her scripture homework last week. Part of it was looking at other faiths like Islam and Hinduism. I told her that followers of those religions will burn in Hell for all eternity as they deny Jesus Christ is our saviour. Now her mum has said that I can't see her any more.
Patrick, 48, Margate

I'm afraid that God and The Devil are engaged in a fight for human souls and I think we know which of them will ultimately claim this unfortunate mother. There is still time for your granddaughter, though. Next time you visit take along some Holy Water in your handbag and perform an improvised baptism. If the mother tries to intervene, simply get out your crucifix and say unto her 'Back, Satan! Oh Lord who is holiest, cast this demon from my presence and let every unclean spirit be repulsed by her.'

If the mum then disappears, screaming in a plume of smoke while sprites fly around her, then you have saved you granddaughter.

If, however, that doesn't happen, it's unlikely you'll be asked to stay for tea.

Well my twenty-three-year-old son, Malcolm, still loves his Lego. Are you suggesting there's something wrong with him? You're no different to all those social workers, psychologists and riot police who all seem to have it in for him. Well, I'm his mother and he's a good boy.
Doreen, 58, Swanage

Actually, Frances, I can assure you that every one of my panty girdles is grass stain free, thank you very much. Perhaps you should stick your bleach up your... *(this letter was cut short for reasons of space)*
Paula, 49, Stevenage

I bought a lovely cuddly zebra for my very first grandson when he was born, but I've never seen it in the baby's nursery. I do feel a bit hurt.
Cathy, 56, Scarborough

It's always upsetting when a present you've lovingly chosen isn't appreciated. It feels like it's *you* who is being rejected as much as the gift. In this case, a good tip is to get a *stuffed* zebra next time, or at least make sure the animal is dead before wrapping it.

I now have nine grandchildren, and they are all adorable, even Chelsea. I love them all, but they are so scared of my husband, Frank that they rarely visit at all these days. I have no idea why as he's never harmed a fly.
Erica, 69, Belfast

It's entirely natural for a child to be a little shy of old people, but for all nine to be terrified suggests that old Frankie boy must have something amiss. When they are due to pop over, try locking Frank in the cellar with a sack over his head so that he doesn't alarm anyone. Make sure you use strong chains to tie him up, and a good set of leg braces might be a wise precaution. If you can, erect an electric fence around him and have a water cannon standing by just in case. Once the grandkids see that he can't escape they'll enjoy playing games with him, or prodding him with sharp sticks if he tries to escape.

I think I had a question about my grandson. Have I already asked it? Did anyone answer?
Arthur, 83, Southampton

Will there be any other questions after mine, only I need to pop to the shop for some suppositories before it closes?
Jean, 59, Welwyn Garden City
No, Jean. Yours is the last one.

Conclusion

Just as the history of Planet Earth can be categorized as a series of geological ages, so your life can be similarly divided.

Both start with a big bang, then a fiery, painful birth, a cooling off period followed by years characterized by reproduction and weathering before the elements cause large cracks to appear and an abundance of fungus in damp, warm places. Then, an unexpected rise in temperature causes all sorts of problems (and flushes) and heralds the final years before the end when they are consumed by fire.

I'm not sure what all this proves, but it does suggest a telling parallel, and that you might need a warmer blanket when you feel your Cretaceous period coming on.

In your short time on this green Earth, you will have young grandchildren for about fifteen of them. Then they reach adulthood, and, if you're not careful, you might end up a footnote in their lives, and the bonds that made you so close, as well as your pelvic floors, will begin to weaken.

So really, this book is about a small percentage of time, even smaller if we're talking geological time, and you need to make the most of it. Because if you do, then your grandchildren will remain close, loving and will visit often to benefit from your accumulated wisdom, love and chocolate brownies.

The cynical reader may think they have detected a common theme running through the pages that can best be summed up as 'your grandchildren are not a good thing and want to wreck your life'.

Nothing could be further from the truth. Being a grandparent is the fulfillment of your life's work, and the time you spend with them will be joyous...*IF* you've been paying attention and don't step on one of the many landmines we've talked about.

Grandparenting takes preparation, practice and hands-on experience. Just like origami or base jumping. If you're not careful, you'll end up with the equivalent of a bin full of strangely folded paper, or a pavement splattered with your intestines.

So even before you are told the wondrous news that a new life has been created, don't leave anything to chance.

Because, unlike that nasty rash on your thigh, your grandchildren are here to stay.

Enjoy.

Appendix: Grandparenting by numbers

42

Percent of Disney baddies who are over the age of fifty-five according to a study of ninety-three characters by Brigham Young University. No wonder your grandchildren are suspicious of you.

9

Percentage of all children in the US who live with their grandparents

Six

The average number of grandchildren per grandparent

500

Hours granny Isobal Varley, 74 has spent being tattooed. She is now in the Guinness Book of Records as the 'World's Most Tattooed Senior Woman', with £20,000 worth of ink covering every inch of her body except her face.

17

Age of the youngest grandmother in history. Mum-Zi, a member of Chief Akkiri's harem on the small island of Calabar, Nigeria, gave birth at 8 years and 4 months. Her daughter then became a mum child at age 8.

29

Age of youngest ever grandfather, Fale Wright, from Warwickshire, England after his son, Stephen's girlfriend gave birth to a baby girl. Fale himself had also become a father at fourteen.

109

Age of the youngest ever great great great great grandmother, Augusta Bunge of Wisconsin, US.

86

Age of oldest grandmother to be tasered by cops in the US. Bedridden Lorna Varner's grandson had called 911 fearing his nan had taken an accidental overdose. But ten policemen showed up and one of them stepped on Lorna's oxygen hose. She then became agitated as she struggled to breathe so the officer zapped her with 50,000 volts. She survived to sue the cops.

45

Percentage of grandparents who use social networking

119

Age of oldest ever great great great great grandmother, Sarah Knauss from Allentown, Pennsylvania. When she died she was the second oldest person ever to have lived and claimed that nibbling on chocolate turtles was her secret to her longevity. Her only daughter was ninety-six when Sarah died, but only made it to one hundred and one, probably ruing the lack of chocolate turtles in her life.

47

Average age of becoming a grandparent

75

Age of sprightly Spain's Got Talent winner, Paddy Jones. The gran won the contest with her energetic flamenco and salsa dancing. She also holds the Guinness record as the oldest acrobatic salsa dancer.

56,000,000

Number of grandparents in the US

64

Average age of all grandparents. The average age that they actually *feel* is more like 94.

£10,000

Amount billionaire Warren Buffett, the world's third richest man, gave each of his grandchildren when they became adults. After that, he told them, they had to make their own way in life.

7,600,000

Google hits for "granny sex". Meanwhile "Grandad sex" only gets 22,900.

30,000

Years ago when Neanderthals first started living until they were old enough to become grandparents, according to fossil records.

4.2

Length in metres of the crocodile Brisbane gran Alicia Sorohan jumped on top of to save her son's mate on a camping trip to Bathurst Bay, Queensland. The 300-kilo saltie had grabbed Andrew Kerr from inside his tent and was dragging him towards the water when plucky Alicia, 61, launched herself onto its back had had her arm nearly ripped off while her son found a gun to shoot it dead.

45

Amount in pounds Man Utd and England striker Wayne Rooney paid to a chain-smoking granny hooker nicknamed the 'Auld slapper' for sex when he was sixteen.

12

Number of years 64-year-old French granny was jailed for castrating her toyboy lover. . . then blaming her dog. The missing manhood was never found.

1980

Year that the film *On Golden Pond* was released starring Henry Fond and Katherine Hepburn. Their characters were voted the Greatest Ever Movie Grandparents by the website grandparents. com. They beat Grandpa Joe from Willy Wonka and the Chocolate Factory into second place. Oddly, Don Corleone also made the top 10.

A third

Percentage of all adults who are grandparents

99

The number of grandchildren and great grandchildren of Hans and Josie Shaffer from Bedford, UK, thought to be a record. The couple had eleven kids and now have fifty-six grandchildren and forty-three great grandchildren. That's a birthday card every three days.

15 million

Number of Google hits for the word 'grandparent'. 'Justin Bieber', by comparison, has 765 million.

100

The age at which Finish grandfather, Eemeli Vayrynen, a prolific inventor, registered his final patent – for a more efficient potato planter.

£30,000

Where bidding reached on ebay when ten-year-old Scot Zoë Pemberton put her granny up for auction. She lovingly described the 61-year-old has 'annoying and moaning a lot'.

Killjoy ebay bosses shut down the sale with the pathetic excuse that ebay doesn't allow human beings to be sold.

40

Percent of Caucasians who have at least some white hair before they are forty.

27

Marathons run on consecutive days by 61-year-old grandmother Rosie Swale Pope from Tenby, West Wales.

38

Percentage of US grandparents who have sex at least twice weekly. Or, possibly more accurately: twice, weakly.

16

Speed in kilometres per hour of the world's slowest police chase, when great gran Caroline Turner, 76, led police on a forty-four kilometer journey in her Ford Fiesta Officers spotted her driving the wrong side of the road in Frinton, England, and tried running alongside her, but she just kept on going.

92

Age of great grandmother, Diane Taylor who was refused alcohol in her local off-licence in Essex, UK because she had no ID to prove she was over eighteen.

35

Percent of women over sixty who are incontinent, which is double the number of men affected.

Acknowledgements

Firstly thanks to my parents for being such an inspiration for this book. In a good way, you understand. And to my wife Ruth who will hopefully stick around when I get grey haired, cranky and require help undressing. That day seems ever more imminent. Finally, my three boys, Joss, Louis and Barney, thank you for prematurely aging me so I *feel* like a grandfather already. And let's make sure I don't become one *just* yet, shall we?

Also by Paul Merrill

HOW TO MUDDLE YOUR WAY THROUGH FATHERHOOD
How to fool people into thinking you're a competent dad...

This is the book dads across the world have been waiting for all their lives, whether they're on the verge of become a dad, or already knee-deep in kids. They just didn't know they were waiting.

Letting you in on the insider secrets the so called 'real' parenting books don't dare tell you, this will arm you with all the tips, cheats and excuses you're going to need to seem like a vaguely competent father.

Find out..

• If you have chosen the right mother for your children
• Simple ways to avoid being assaulted during childbirth
• Why babies shouldn't watch Schindler's List
• How to change a nappy in 17 easy stages
• Coping strategies for if your son becomes a nerd
• The greatest lies to tell your kids
• How can you make your child less stupid?
• Tell-tale signs your teenager has become a terrorist

Using a series of scientifically questionable quizzes, flowcharts, checklists and celebrity advice, this award-worthy book will quite possibly be the most important thing you ever read and will ensure that no one thinks you're a terrible father again. Except possibly your kids, but they don't count.

Follow Paul at @paulmerrill68

Made in the USA
Middletown, DE
18 December 2016